In Press.

TRAGEDY OF ERRORS.

RECORD

OF

AN OBSCURE MAN.

"Aux plus déshérités le plus d'amour."

BOSTON:
TICKNOR AND FIELDS.
1861.

RIVERSIDE, CAMBRIDGE:
STEREOTYPED AND PRINTED BY H. O. HOUGHTON.

RECORD OF AN OBSCURE MAN.

I.

In the spring of 1842 I made a tour through some of the Southern and Southwestern States. I travelled chiefly on horseback, — partly for health, partly on account of the greater opportunity thus afforded for those way-side adventures which give such a zest to the rambles of a young man journeying without any definite object. I met with many, — some piquant enough, others far from charming. But all seem pleasant in the distance; and these, my earliest travelling-experiences, furnished me long, and furnish me still, with stuff for many an after-dinner story and many an evening reverie.

Among the incidents of this youthful excursion was one of the more quiet sort, to which my thoughts have reverted oftener than to the many comic adventures or even to the hair-breadth escapes that have entertained my listeners. Yet, up to this time, it has been shared with no one. I now first break the seal of silence which some feeling inexplicable to myself has laid upon my lips, and open at once to the great public a corner of my life into which neither intimate acquaintance nor trusted friend has hitherto looked.

At the close of an April day, hotter than in the North we often know in June, I was surprised by one of those sudden storms of rain and lightning so common in Southern regions. The night came on prematurely, bringing with it a thick darkness that might be felt. This, taking turns with the frequent blaze of blinding lightning, at length completely bewildered and discouraged me, tired as I was, and following a strange road, with no very clear idea of my place of destination. I let my horse take his own way, and, sitting listlessly in the saddle, judged of our progress and of the nature of the route only by the sound of the poor beast's feet, as they sank softly in the moist sand, or·plashed in the swollen torrents that now and then burst across the path.

I had gone forward in this way for about an hour, when I was roused from my half-stupor by the sudden stopping of my horse. I looked up, and saw near me on the right a friendly glimmer, sent, apparently, from the window of a not distant house, of which a flash of lightning soon gave me a more distinct view. When the peal of thunder had died away, I lifted up my voice; for a fence lay between me and the promised shelter; and the lightning, now less frequent, hardly sufficed to guide me to the entrance. My appeal was not lost. The light on which my eyes were fixed moved; a window was heard to open. I repeated my call; but, before I had time to explain my situation, the window was hastily closed, and in another moment a light was seen moving from the direction of the house and coming by a somewhat circuitous path towards me. The bearer soon reached me, guided by my voice, and, with a simple "Good evening," spoken in a tone which assured me I had fallen into no unfriendly hands, opened the gate against which my horse was already pressing. The gleam of the lantern led me through the black darkness to the house. My guide threw open the door, as I somewhat slowly brought to the ground my cramped and dripping limbs, and, leaving me to find my way by myself, led off my horse, whose lively step betrayed that he hailed the prospect of a shelter with as much satisfaction as his master. I eagerly gained the doorway, through which the light streamed invitingly; but paused when I had passed the threshold, and turned quickly to close the door and exclude the damp night-wind.

The most conspicuous object in the room I had entered was a low couch, on which was extended a woman, whose pale features I saw distinctly by the light of the lamp which stood on a little table near her. She was giving directions to a black woman who was busy near the fire, which, to my great contentment, glowed on the wide hearth. I was struck, even in the moment of entering, by the gentleness of the speaker's voice, contrasting, as it did, with the imperious tones to which my ear had become habituated during the weeks I had passed in the Southern country. As I hesitated to advance, she addressed me with courtesy and invited me to approach the fire. I obeyed her gladly. The black woman, who, on my sudden entrance, had advanced into the middle of the floor, had stood erect and watchful, until she saw the impression made on her mistress by the new guest. She now returned to the hearth, and, after a quick glance of inspection, offered me welcome in her turn by heaping wood on the fire. The blaze rose high, and, through its influence, I had already sufficiently recovered myself, by the time our host reëntered, to return with grateful cordiality the greeting he offered me.

My till now unseen friend was a man a little above the middle height, apparently about thirty years of age. He had in his appearance and manners little of the backwoodsman and still less of the small planter. He wore a blouse of homely material, confined round the waist by a leathern belt. This rude costume — about that time much affected on summer excursions by young men of fashion in the Northern and Middle States — had, on his erect and slender figure, a certain picturesque grace, and seemed rather to have been assumed through caprice than worn as matter of custom and necessity. Having offered me welcome, he forestalled my inquiries by assuring me of the well-being of my horse. He had brought with him my saddle-bags, and invited me to follow him to an upper room where I could relieve myself of my wet garments. A steep, narrow staircase, or rather a sort of ladder, led to this room, which was evidently his own. As my bags could not be supposed to contain a very extensive wardrobe, he took from a trunk and offered me a linen blouse of the same fashion with that which he wore, but of finer material. Requesting me to make use of any other article I might need, he left me. From the open trunk rose the fresh odor of the herbs which old-fashioned New England housewives dispose between the layers of newly washed linen. The wholesome fragrance carried me back to the happiest, freest days of my childhood, — those days of vacation passed on the ancestral farm, under the gentle control of my patient grandmother. I stood again in the low room, before the great oaken chest-of-drawers. I heard the whispering of the poplars that bordered the terraced garden, and the tap of the woodpecker in the elm whose remaining half shaded the rustic well. The illusion, transient as it was, lent something home-like and familiar to my temporary shelter. The feelings it had called up had hardly passed away when I joined my host in the lower room.

I found the supper-table spread. I was invited to take my place at it in the most comfortable chair the house afforded. I now felt sufficiently at ease to take a survey of the apartment and its furniture. Both were of an humble character. But perfect neatness and order prevailed; and over all was diffused an air of comfort which I had often missed in the more sumptuous mansions I had visited in my tour, and which I had not before met with in the houses of persons of the class to which I must suppose my entertainers belonged. The table, with its glossy cloth, its bright knives, and the unusual luxury of napkins, resembled little the often profuse, but always ill-appointed board of the Southern petty land-owner. The quality of the viands differed as much from that of those to which I had of late been accustomed as the manner of serving them did. The bread was of Indian corn,—a material which, according to the mode of preparation, may furnish delicacies for the fastidious, or the most repulsive food that ever hunger satisfied itself upon. I had lately had abundant experience of this grain under its least attractive form. On the present occasion it made its appearance under that of the lightest and most delicate of biscuit, with which the dish was constantly replenished by the solicitous Tabitha, — for this, I found, was the name of the stately black woman, who, with a full sense of their importance, filled the posts of cook and waiter.

The invalid, from her couch, superintended the operations near the fire. Each dish was, in its turn, submitted to her inspection before being placed on the table. All the directions were given in the same quiet tone which I had remarked on my first entrance. I now observed that her voice, though low, was clear and musical and had nothing of the feebleness of ill-health. Yet her white, thin hands, her transparent skin, and the expression of patience stamped upon her worn features, told of protracted suffering.

My host did the honors with perfect courtesy. We did not, howèver, make much progress in each other's acquaintance. His manner was frank and cordial, but he spoke little, and, contrary to the custom of the region in which he lived, neither asked me questions about my affairs, nor volunteered information in regard to his own. On my part, I, who like well enough the communicativeness of our Southern and Western brothers, and who am of opinion that what concerns one human being ought not to be indifferent to any other, felt myself a little damped by a reserve to which I had disaccustomed myself since I left home. In fact, when I drew my chair up to the table, I had indulged in a full expectation of that exchange of confidences which usually took place between the guest and his entertainer under similar circumstances. I was ready to tell as much about myself as my companion could desire to hear, and was prepared to learn from him in return all I wished to know, namely: his name; his place of birth; what brought him here; who the lady on the couch was, and what relation she bore to him. The supper passed, however, without the satisfaction of my curiosity, or, apparently, the excitement of his. Our conversation was of the most general character. It related chiefly to the productions of the country, its climate, and so forth. I should, perhaps, in my wearied state, have found it tedious, if my fancy, on the alert for indications to guide it, had not kept up a running commentary and found romantic suggestions in the most prosaic statements.

Fatigue, however, at length got the better of curiosity. The game of reply and rejoinder flagged, and at last ceased altogether. My host, in answer to my tired look, took up a candle and offered to conduct me to my sleeping-room. We mounted the ladder to the chamber into which I had before been introduced, and from which the articles of dress that had hung upon the walls had disappeared. I saw very well that my host was depriving himself of his room for my accommodation, but a feeling of shyness which had crept over me prevented me from making known to him my recognition of this act of hospitality. He cast a look of inspection about the room, and then, as if satisfied that all was in order, wished me a good night, extending, after a moment's hesitation, his hand, and grasping mine cordially as he saw the motion promptly and warmly met on my part. A bright smile lighted up his face at the same time, and he left with me the pleasant consciousness that I was not regarded as an intrusive or an unwelcome guest.

Notwithstanding my hospitable entertainment, I did not entirely escape the consequences of the exposure I had suffered. The fresh, cool bed invited to the sleep my fatigue rendered necessary. But I courted it in vain. I lay tranquil, but sleepless, my ear taking in the sounds that came to it from the lower room. In this way I assisted at the clearing of the supper-table, and the consequent household rites, indicated by an alternate clatter and splash. As these began, I heard the outer door open and close, and followed the footsteps of my friend, on his way, I made no doubt, to the cattle-shed. I then recollected, with a qualm of conscience, that, for the first time in my rambles, my absorption in myself, or my confidence in the hospitality of the house that had received me, or both together, had made me forget to look after the supper and bedding of my horse. I was half-inclined to rise; but my weariness, and the assurance I felt that my host had gone out to atone for my neglect, persuaded me to content myself where I was. The sounds that soon came to me from without, and which I easily interpreted, following in imagination the processes they indicated, confirmed my impression, — as the ejaculations, now encouraging, now admonitory, in which men communicate with the dependent animals, met my ear, accompanied by a patter of horses' feet, and now and then a snort or grateful whinny.

Within the house, in the mean time, the evening duties went on. Their fulfilment was cheered and the various sounds composed by a low chant, which I at once referred to Tabitha. In its suppressed tones, which now and then broke through their restraint to be instantly subdued again, I perceived the deference paid to the unseen presence of a stranger. The last clash of crockery and the last notes of the melody died away together, and a grand opening and shutting of drawers announced the finale of the evening's performances, when the outer door again opened, to admit the master of the house. After his return, a moving of chairs and tables, then the opening and closing of a door or two, and then profound quiet.

This seemed hardly to be broken, when, shortly after, the low, continuous murmur of a voice made itself heard. I inferred, from the uniformity of the tone, that it was the voice of some one reading aloud. My first impression was that the master of the house was beguiling the weary hours for the sufferer on the couch; but I soon perceived that the voice was not that of a man, and, listening more attentively, I thought I could recognize the low, sweet accents of the invalid herself. I tried to soothe myself by the lulling sound and to escape into sleep by its aid, but in vain. It ceased at last. The night was already far advanced. The storm was over. The stars twinkled on me through the cracks in the roof above my head. I watched their glimmer until it faded out before the light of day.

I now gave up the thought of sleep, and, weary of my useless imprisonment, resolved to rise. It was then I first became aware that my strength had been fearfully reduced during this watchful night. On my first essay, I fell back helpless. It was only after repeated efforts that I succeeded.

I would not go down until summoned; for the staircase led immediately into the room where we had supped, and I felt that the presence of a stranger at that early hour must be inconvenient in an apartment which served so many purposes. I looked round for something to divert myself with until the hour of breakfast. I wandered to the window. The view from it was tame and did not hold me long. Some young trees gave promise for the future, but the land had been pitilessly cleared.

I then turned my observation upon the room. It was still ruder in finish and in furniture than that below. The chairs and bedstead were evidently of domestic manufacture. A case of shelves, protected by a curtain of wall-paper made to roll up by a simple contrivance, was plainly of the same workmanship. I discovered that this supplied the place of a wardrobe. As my eye thus took account of the objects in the room, it fell upon one which gave evidence of a certain luxury nowhere else visible. In the end farthest from that at which I was seated, hung from a black and gilt cornice a silk curtain with draperies profuse in fringe and tassels. It seemed to cover a wide door or alcove, or perhaps only the front of a large piece of furniture. I looked at it for some time with a languid curiosity, which, gradually becoming more lively, at last drew me to examine it. I found what seemed at first a wide wardrobe or book-case, of which the sides were ornamented with Japan work, — a black ground with raised figures of birds and flowers in gold and brilliant colors. I drew aside one half of the curtain, which opened in the middle, and found that it concealed a large recess, of which the ornamented woodwork formed the doorway. This recess, unlike the chamber, which was open to the roof, had a plastered ceiling. With the exception of a slit cut to receive the narrow window that lighted it, the little cabinet was entirely lined with books. They were nearly all covered with stout paper, and, on taking some of them down, I found the additional precaution of a paper case which protected the edges of the leaves. The other furniture of the recess consisted of an old-fashioned high-backed arm-chair, and a little table with writing-materials, which stood before it. I seated myself in the chair and amused myself with reading the titles of the books. They were of the most varied description, and were arranged according to their subject, without reference to their size or the language in which they were written. In this little repository almost all times and nations had their representatives. I found a good collection of classic authors, the masters of modern literature in all the tongues with which I was acquainted, many books offering combinations of letters strange to my eye, and others in characters wholly unknown to me.

Then there were volumes which, though no great connoisseur in these matters, I could easily perceive, from the date of the printing and the beauty of the type, to be rare editions. There seemed to be no luxury of binding, except in the case of some of these old books, which had perhaps once held their place in some princely library.

In most of the books I opened was written the name, — Edward Colvil; in a few, that of Harriet Colvil. In some of them both these names were found. Were they those of my host and hostess?

The interest I found in searching among these hidden treasures suspended for a time the sense of feebleness which had oppressed me when I rose, but it soon returned and weighed upon me doubly. I tried to read, but gave it up and tottered to the bed, where my host, when he came to call me to breakfast, found me stretched, indifferent to everything.

Five days I was held there, during which time my new friend treated me in conformity with the prescriptions given by the mistress of the house, who, from her couch, now superintended the progress of my cure, as she had done the preparations for my supper on the evening of my arrival.

My host, in administering her remedies, spoke of her as his mother. Each time that he pronounced this name, his voice lowered with an involuntary accent of tenderness and respect that impressed me and increased my desire to know something more of her history and his.

On the sixth day I was well enough to leave my room. Early in the afternoon I was aided down the difficult stairway by my good host, and once more installed in the chair of honor, mine by the double title of guest and invalid. The mistress of the house addressed to me some words of simple kindness which set me at my ease, and then took up the needlework with which she had been engaged when I entered. She was, as before, reclining upon her couch, and I observed that she drew out her needle slowly and with an appearance of exertion. She addressed her son as Edward. The Edward Colvil of the books, of course. I was glad to have a name to call him by in my thoughts, but I could not venture to address him by it without some more decisive authority. During the hours he had passed in my sick-room, Edward had read to me, had talked with me over a wide range of subjects, historical, political, literary; but had let fall nothing that had reference to his past life or present occupations and circumstances. Had this silence been reserve or delicacy? I risked an essay.

"Are you not from New England?"

"Yes, from Massachusetts."

And here he stopped. I waited a little, but nothing more came. Edward seemed rather thrown into thought by my question, than stimulated to talk. I took up the word again myself.

"I was born in New England."

"I saw the New-Englander in you at once," said Edward's mother, looking towards me, as I thought, very kindly.

The friendly smile with which Edward regarded me was his only answer. They were no more solicitous, it seemed, to know more about me than to tell me more about themselves. Once launched, however, I went forward. I had soon told them where I was born, where I lived, who my parents were, and what I was travelling about for, — all without their helping me very much with their questions. They showed, however, as much interest as I could desire. I gradually opened myself more and more, and, as the current of sympathy became established between us, they led me on by their pleased attention and discriminating comments till I had related more of myself and my family-affairs than I should beforehand have thought judicious to confide to strangers. I even wandered back into traditional family-anecdotes, and had just arrived at the knight of Malta whom we count among the collateral honors of our family-tree, when I was checked by a sudden misgiving that I was making myself ridiculous. I saw, however, no signs of such an impression on the part of my listeners. On the contrary, the kindness they had hitherto shown me seemed warmed into an almost affectionate familiarity after these confidences.

By the time the sun went down and the evening fire was kindled I felt as one of the family, and even ventured to aid in some little offices which in this small household claimed the personal attention of the master. In this way I cleared from the table, about to be arranged for supper, some objects that incumbered it,—among them a book or two, which, after having placed the other things in safety on the shelves with which the walls were furnished, I permitted myself to retain.

"You allow me?" I said to Edward, as I opened one of them.

"Certainly. They are the books in which my mother was reading to me last evening."

"Your mother reads German, then?" I asked, in some surprise.

"Yes, she learned it in order to read to me."

Edward went on to tell me that he had some years before been attacked by a complaint of the eyes which threatened to hinder the prosecution of his studies. He was then at an age when an interruption is fatal. His mother had done all that was possible, and almost the impossible, to mitigate to him the effects of his misfortune. She read to him, during the hours he had hitherto been able to devote to study, in English and in other languages. French and Italian she already possessed. Of German she learned from him the principles of the pronunciation, and attempted at first to read to him without herself understanding what she was imparting; but finding that the false expression and emphasis into which she unavoidably fell detracted from the pleasure of listening, and even sometimes rendered it a fatigue, she set resolutely about the study of the language, and was now able to enjoy with her son the treasures it holds. I learned further that the faithful mother had for many years been held, by one of those obscure diseases which pass under the name of spine-complaints, almost helpless to her couch, and it was there she had pursued these studies in the moments she could abstract from her necessary needlework and the superintendence of the housekeeping, from which duties her infirm condition did not exempt her. I gathered that she had, at some previous period of her life, either from poverty or some other cause, been compelled for a length of time to make exertions greatly beyond her strength, and that to these the malady which had crippled her was attributable.

Interested as I was in my new friends, and desirous of further confidences, I would willingly have prolonged my evening in their company. But this was not permitted me. The signs of lassitude, which I had endeavored to suppress, were quickly detected by my hostess. Perhaps her own experience had quickened her perceptions. She early reminded her son that I was an invalid, and, when I sincerely expressed my wish to remain longer with them, overruled it with decision. Edward aided me to my room and left me, promising to return later in the evening to see if I had need of anything. He came accordingly. I was not asleep, and begged him to sit down by me. He complied; and then, without preamble, I asked him to tell me something more of his past history. There was nothing in it very romantic, after all.

He was the son of a clergyman of New England, whom ill-health had compelled to leave his parish and his native State. The mildness of the climate and some accidental circumstances had decided him to settle in the place where his wife and son still lived. He had invested the greater part of his little property in the land and the buildings erected upon it. He did not long enjoy his estate. The benefit he derived from change of climate was more than counterbalanced by the hardships and fatigues of his new life. Accustomed to purely intellectual pursuits, the necessity of turning his attention to material wants and occupying himself with the grosser cares of life harassed and disgusted him. He was not able to conceal the disappointment he suffered in this strange land, which he had pictured to himself beforehand as an earthly paradise, and for whose soft air he had longed in his wintry birthplace as for the fountain of youth and health. His wife and children did all in their power to support the failing man, and to avert from him fatigue and anxiety. But the restlessness of disease and of dissatisfaction drove him to seek the exertions that wasted him. He sank after a few painful years. The management of the little farm, which had been, at least ostensibly, conducted by the father, devolved upon Edward, then not twenty years of age. He was at that time aided by two younger brothers.

The mother, now the sole guardian of the little exiled family, exerted herself not only to maintain order and comfort for her children, but to obviate, as far as possible, the disadvantages of a removal from cultivated society and public means of education. She strove to keep alive in her sons the tastes awakened in former years, and to stimulate in them the desire of knowledge. She would not suffer them to give their whole time to manual labor, but engaged them to set apart a certain portion of the day for reading and study in common. This custom, at first, at least on the part of the younger sons, a sacrifice to filial piety, acquired the force of a religious observance; as did also the habits of neatness and order, which respect for this tender mother prevailed on them to maintain, in spite of the temptations to neglect them which their isolated and difficult life offered, — temptations under the force of which so many of the emigrants from civilized into newly settled countries relapse into barbarism.

His two brothers Edward described to me as noble boys, contrasts to each other in appearance and character, but both lovely and both highly gifted in their different ways. They fell victims to the cholera, which for two successive seasons ravaged the country. It was after the death of the second, that the forces of the mother, which she had long maintained only by the energy of her spirit, failed her at once. About a year before this misfortune, a free black woman, whose entire family had been carried off by the cholera, had come to the house of the Colvils to ask a home. She had been kindly received, and had been instructed in the careful performance of household duties, in preparation for finding her a more lucrative service. This woman, who proved intelligent and faithful, seeing that her protectress was likely to have need of her, declared her firm resolution never to leave her. She remained accordingly, and had proved herself a devoted nurse to her mistress, who, through her, was enabled to keep up the order and neatness which had always marked her housekeeping.

"Tabitha is not a slave, then?"

"Oh, no!"

Edward seemed surprised at the question.

"And do you carry on your farm, likewise, without slave-labor?"

"Certainly. I have been so fortunate as to engage the services of a German and his sons. The father does not understand English, so that I have an opportunity of speaking German. He is not without education, and has a pretty good accent. I give the sons lessons in English, and even by this I learn something, so that I have a double advantage in employing them. In the busier seasons I engage some occasional labor, which is always to be obtained from the emigrants who are constantly passing through our State. Our worthy German has put up a house, and has fully established himself here with his family."

I remembered to have heard, during my confinement to my bed, the tones of a male voice of a different quality from Edward's, and to have seen a broad back disappearing through the door when I went down in the morning.

Reserve being now at an end, I asked Edward some questions in regard to his family. I found that he was of the stock of the New England Pilgrims, — of that most respectable of emigrations, composed of men that had known neither the deterioration which want causes, nor that consequent on intercourse with a court. I have no portion in the Pilgrim Fathers, but I have not the less a filial regard for them, and felt my respect for Edward Colvil increased when I knew he was of their blood. I expressed this to him, and felicitated him on his connection with those erect and independent men, the truest representatives of the English nation, uniting the sturdiness of the peasant with the cultivation of the gentleman. He accepted my congratulations frankly, but was not quite so ready to expatiate on the subject of his lineage as I had shown myself in regard to mine.

By a little persistence, however, I discovered that he was a true New-Englander in his respect for genealogy. I was well pleased to lead him into disclosures in this direction, and all the more because I had a misgiving that I had a little paraded the honors of my own family-tree. He made no pretension to anything very illustrious. He was derived on both sides from families whose records had been carefully kept for centuries. They were, like those of my own family, graced by some moderate celebrities, but could boast no names supereminent either in genius or in crime, — in short, gave occasion for no livelier feeling than the quiet satisfaction found in an honorable and unblemished descent. As is the case with most New-Englanders, many different races had a share in him. Welsh, Saxon, Norman, Scotch, and Norwegian blood met in his veins. We are apt, of the many rivulets that furnish the tide of our life, to choose out some one source as the subject of more special self-gratulation. I found he was no exception here, but that, even as I find my highest pride in my Gaelic lineage, so he held most dear his Scandinavian blood. Perhaps it was because he had it from his mother. Yet it was not conspicuous in him. She showed her Northern descent in her white, transparent skin and calm blue eyes. His rapidly varying complexion and the changeful expression of his dark eyes spoke of the inheritance of a temperament fostered by warmer suns. It came, perhaps, from the sensitive, melancholic father.

Before we parted for the night the intimacy between us was fully established. I did not hesitate to tell him of the inroad I had made on the first morning into his little sanctum, and expressed my curiosity in regard to the exceptional luxury that surrounded it. I found that it had been arranged during the lifetime of the father, by the care of his affectionate wife and children, who had endeavored to soothe his sick spirit by every appliance within their reach. The curtains, Edward told me, were an heirloom, and had once hung in the parlor of his mother's grandmother. He remembered that in his childhood they were kept in an oaken chest in which they had been preserved since the time of the Revolution, when his great-grandfather, who was a Tory, was obliged to leave the country. They had always been looked on with respect by the family; and when, at the time of their migration, the necessary division was made between the articles of furniture to be sacrificed and those that were to be forwarded to the new home, these, with the high-backed chair, — a Puritan relic, — and the old-fashioned couch in the lower room, were reserved by general consent. The Japan painting of the frame and cornice was his mother's work. She had not herself beforehand a very correct idea of the life she was to lead, or of its exactions, and had brought with her the material for various kinds of fancy-work which had been the recreation of her youth, and for which she expected to have abundant time in her quiet country-home. The last and only use she made of these little accomplishments was in the garnishing of her husband's "study," as the little nook was called in which the remnant of his library was stored up. For, though they had brought with them little luxury of furniture, they had preserved their most valuable books and those that would be most useful in the education of their children. These formed the nucleus of the present collection.

II.

When Edward came to call me the next morning, he invited me, before going down, to take a look at his little study. I saw that philology was his favorite pursuit. He first directed my attention to the shelves on which the great lights of this science reposed. But when he perceived that their names did not precisely awaken enthusiasm in me, he pointed out his collection of dramatic writers. "It is incomplete," he said, "but it contains nearly all that I could want to read more than once, and I cannot afford to own books that will bear only a single reading." In historical works his little treasury seemed rich. I found the books were put up in double, sometimes in triple rows; so that the collection was, in fact, much larger than it at first appeared.

Most of the books in foreign living languages had been procured by Edward on his occasional visits to the nearest large city. He was in the habit of leaving his orders with the principal bookseller there, and was often obliged to wait many months, sometimes even a year, before the long-desired book came into his possession. He did not tell me at that time by what exertions and what self-denial the acquisition of these books had been attained; but I almost divined it when he showed me some catalogues of German booksellers in which he had marked the titles of certain books with three crosses, others with two, others again with one, according to the degree of his desire for them. When circumstances permitted the purchase of a book, one of the triply marked was selected, and so on in order of interest. When I saw how many were marked with the threefold cross of honor without having yet received the fourth, which indicated their final promotion to the chosen society on his shelves, I could not help regarding Edward with a momentary compassion. But then again, remarking the bright expectant smile with which he enjoyed in advance his future conquests, as he glanced from page to page of his catalogue, I felt that he could not have had more pleasure from his authors, and probably would not have read them half so thoroughly, if he could have had a large library for the wishing. A row of books bound uniformly, in a very simple way, and not, like the others, protected by paper, caught my eye. They were manuscript copies, made by himself, of works difficult to be obtained, that had been lent to him, or that he had found in the public libraries, on his rare visits to the Eastern cities. The somewhat rude binding was his own handiwork.

I asked him whether he possessed the key to the strange tongues in which some of his books were written, and how he had obtained it. He told me he had begun the study of these languages by himself, aided by good grammars in German ; that in most of them he had received assistance from some of those wandering teachers whom Europe's misfortunes send us. Emigrants of various nations, of all conditions, and all degrees of education, passed through this region on their way to a still more attractive and more Southern country. They were often glad to accept the offered hospitality of a few days' or weeks' repose, and give in return what they had, in default of silver and gold.

When we went down to the lower room, we found everything in order and the breakfast awaiting us. The mother reclined as usual on her couch, which, with its heavy black wood and the pale green damask of its many cushions, had an Old-World air very pleasant in a region where the works of man were so recent. It seemed that its occupant must feel less banished, supported by this relic of an older home. She greeted me kindly, as I entered with her son, and joined occasionally in our conversation during breakfast. Her delicate, tremulous hands were already employed upon her ceaseless needlework.

The day was rainy. It was decided that I was not to venture out; but Edward, seeing that I was well enough to amuse myself by reading, did not offer to remain with me. He referred me to the books on the small table near his mother, or to those in the study above, for my morning's entertainment, and then, without further apology than that some matters without required his attention, left me.

I thought it expedient to return to my room; for I foreboded that the one in which we had breakfasted must be for some time the scene of household duties which did not invite my coöperation. I requested, however, permission of my hostess to return at a later hour and bring with me a volume of poems from which I proposed to read to her some of my favorite pieces.

I found she was acquainted with the name of the author, but not yet with his works, with the exception of a few poems that had found their way into the newspapers. I was pleased to see her mild blue eyes brighten and deepen at the prospect of the entertainment I offered her. She promised to let me know as soon as all should be in order for my reception.

The summons came, after a not very long interval, during which I had been made aware of an extraordinary alacrity on the part of Tabitha, who, to judge by the vivacity of her movements, sympathized keenly in the anticipations of her mistress.

There was a slight flush on the usually white cheek of the invalid, and an almost tremulous expectation visible on her features, as I opened the volume. A new book makes an epoch in the lives of the isolated dwellers in newly settled countries. My listener prepared herself for attention by resuming the work she had dropped for a moment on my entrance. I read her one of the shorter poems in the volume, then, after a little pause, a second, and after another interval, a third. She made no remark, and gave no sign of applause, other than that implied by the occasional dropping of her work and the fixing of her eyes upon me with a look of rapt attention. I avoided that fatal question, "How do you like it?" the so frequent extinguisher of enthusiasm, and waited in silence a signal to go on.

Tabitha, in the mean while, seated near the head of her mistress's couch, and supposed to be occupied with some piece of work, which I fear did not prosper much, kept time, with a backward and forward movement of the head, to the cadence of the verse. Even when the reading had ceased, she continued this sympathetic motion, as if the melody still lingered in her ear.

"You have given me a great pleasure," said the invalid at last, and then relapsed into meditation, which I did not interrupt. When she turned toward me with an expression that implied she was ready to hear more, I read again; and again paused.

"You will permit my son to copy some of these poems?" she said, on returning to herself, after another interval of abstraction.

"No,—I will leave the volume with you, when I go."

"Oh!" in an accent of deep satisfaction. This was her acceptance of my offer, without other thanks.

I had never been so fully sensible of the power of genius as when I saw its magic exerted in that rude, lonely dwelling, freeing the helpless sufferer from her pains and cares. What a benefaction of Heaven is this gift! No wonder its possessors think they have enough and are negligent of this world's goods. What could wealth add to the privileges of genius? To the ambitious it gives power the most real,—that over the soul; to the lover of praise, the purest glory; to the benevolent, the means of benefiting thousands. I expressed something of this to Mrs. Colvil. She assented warmly.

"Yes, — and in the pursuit of wealth, or of the high station which alone can give the extended influence that genius commands, what temptations to be encountered! how many mean cares! how many petty contests! The man who has begun his career with the purest aims, by the time he has obtained the means to carry them out, has, perhaps, already lost sight of them. The man of letters, while preparing for his career, and while pursuing it, may possess his soul in peace. And then what happiness there must be in the consciousness of a sacred gift treasured up until the fitting moment, and then given forth, blessing and enriching! Yes, — I believe the poet who devotes all his powers to the service of God must be the happiest of men."

As she said this, in her low, feeling voice, a soft smile played on her face, called forth by some thought inly cherished. She spoke rather as if considering the subject within herself than as if addressing me. But she turned towards me, as she ceased, with a look of inquiry.

"You ought to be right," I said; "and yet, after all, we are apt to associate the thought of morbid sensitiveness, of melancholy, of disappointment, with genius."

"Is it not when it has been profaned to serve a worldly ambition or a selfish vanity, that the sacred fire consumes, instead of animating?"

"Perhaps so. But the man of letters has, then, his temptations, as well as the aspirant for wealth or place?"

She was silent for a few moments, and then said absently, —

"There are characters, however, not subject to these temptations."

"Men of genius exempt from them are rare. And are they not, in this case, apt to rest content with dreams and wishes? It seems as if a certain amount of alloy were needed to fit the fine gold for earthly use."

She appeared struck by this suggestion.

"Yes. And then the self-distrust, the conscientiousness, even, of sensitive natures, often holds them back. Ambition and love of praise are keen spurs. But then," she added, recovering herself, "may not the desire of doing good be a passion as strong as either of these?"

"As strong, perhaps, but hardly so lively or so impulsive."

"And the indignation against wrong?"

"That is sometimes a powerful propeller, certainly."

"Oh," she exclaimed, with sudden animation,

"I believe, and you believe, I am sure, that there are characters which know no hatred but that of wrong, and whose strongest passion is the love of right!"

I did not answer, for I had never precisely considered the question.

"My son is of these. The thirst for knowledge and the desire of doing good are the strongest forces in him, and I can see that the latter is gradually gaining the ascendancy over the former."

The effects of an isolated life in a new settlement, upon persons accustomed to cultivated society, are very various. Some yield at once to the influences of their new position, and soon show no traces of former refinement. On others is stamped the exasperation of futile regrets that accompany the progress of deterioration without giving the force to resist it. There are others in whom the old life and the new harmonize, instead of clashing, and who seem to have drawn into their natures the best elements of both: the amenity of manners remains, the graceful deference to the feelings of others, while what is merely conventional and external has passed away, leaving a childlike simplicity and directness, a perfect openness in word and deed, which, when met with in persons of forcible character and expanded intellect, has a charm not to be resisted.

I had already seen examples of this combination of the refinement of civilization with the frankness of primitive life; and I was the less surprised that Mrs. Colvil should thus think aloud before me, for I saw that her last words were the continuation of an inward train of thought. I followed it up quickly to its source and came upon a discovery.

"Your son is an author?"

"Not yet."

"He intends to be?"

"I should rather say hopes than intends, — perhaps rather desires than hopes."

"It was of his career, then, you were thinking? It was to him you were wishing this happiness of benefiting thousands?" I said, deeply moved as I looked upon this infirm woman, whose soul embraced the world in its love. Tears gathered in my eyes as I spoke. She saw them gratefully.

"Since he first saw the light," she said, after a short hesitation, "the wish has been in my heart that he might not leave the world without its being a little better for his having been in it. He is the only one remaining to me of three sons, for all of whom I have offered the same prayer. God may remove him, too, to another sphere before he has accomplished any visible work in this; but if his life is prolonged" ——

She paused, as if she shrank from embodying in words hopes so sacred, yet perhaps so baseless.

"But you will think my presumption greater than it is. I do not know how I have been led to say so much. I know the disadvantages that Edward has suffered under: his irregular education; the want of the means of instruction found in the older States; the further deprivation caused by the weakness of his sight for many years. I know, too, that more is required now to make a poet than a lively imagination and a rhythmical ear. Yet, with all this, I believe that a man who feels the impulse to write, and who writes in earnest of what he has himself seen and felt, will find, in our wide country, those who need and will listen to what he has to say."

"Your son has, perhaps, already written?"

"I am betraying Edward's secret. But why should I not to you?"

There was something in that *you* that thrilled me with a sense of new pleasure. It is a moment of high satisfaction in the life of a man whose path has lain along the beaten track, and who has found his associates among the practical, not to say the worldly, when he first meets with the recognition of his claim to the freedom of another community, and, half-doubting, half-exulting, descends into his own spirit and discovers depths of which he has been dimly aware, but which he has never ventured to explore. This pleasure came to me first in that lonely farm-house, in the society of the infirm widow and her son. I was the child of wealthy parents. From my earliest youth everything had been in my power,—everything that riches could give. I was well liked in society, for I was free-handed and easy-tempered. But no one regarded me as a man of deep feeling, nor did I regard myself as such. Yet I was conscious of something within me that had never been put to use, and that was always seeking to find its office. This deeper side of my nature, as it first opened itself to my friends of the wilderness, so they alone have had the key to it. It has remained closed to human eye since the grave closed over them. As regards the world in which I have held my daily walk, I have gone through life thus far, and shall go to the end, with the reputation of a superficial man.

"*But why should I not to you?*" The emotions and thoughts which this question called up glanced rapidly through me and did not suspend my answer.

"It will be safe in my keeping. You will let me see some of his writings?"

"I should be most glad to have your opinion of them,—if only Edward consent. But he must consent; for how can he ever find courage to submit his works to the great indifferent public, if he shrink from trusting them to the eye of a friend?"

"He has not published anything, then?"

"He has not yet found confidence. He knows that self-delusion on such a subject is easy. He has read his writings with no one but me, and he fears my judgment is too indulgent."

"He has no friends, then, in the neighborhood?"

"He has acquaintances among the owners of the nearest plantations, and some of them are well-qualified to judge of a literary work. They seem to value his society, and constantly invite him to their houses; but he has never formed such an intimacy with any of them as could enable him to lay aside his diffidence and break silence on such a subject. He has, indeed, a friend, tutor on a plantation about twenty miles distant, in whom he could confide. But, though this friend has much sympathy with Edward on some points, on others he is quite incapable of comprehending him. He is insensible to poetry, and has no belief in its power to effect anything."

I read again; but I soon perceived that I was no longer listened to with undivided attention. The mother's eyes were raised from her work and fixed on me at times as before, — yet not, as before, with an intelligent, sympathetic glance, but rather as if they wandered, impelled by some inward excitement. The slender fingers trembled, as they set the hesitating needle. She was thrilling with the future of her son; or perhaps her tremor was caused only by the thought of the near ordeal she had prepared for him, though it was formidable only because the first.

I did not let her see that I had remarked her abstraction, but silently suffered my book to sink and then to close. Tabitha took immediate advantage of this pause, for which she had perhaps been waiting with impatience. A sudden rattling of tongs and shovel, and banging of cooking-utensils drawn from their lurking-places by her vigorous hand, recalled her mistress to the every-day world and its cares. Her glance was directed first to the clock, then rested for an instant with approbation upon Tabitha, before it fell again on me.

"You are tired," she exclaimed, as she noticed my indolent attitude; and an expression of alarm clouded her face, as if she feared she had permitted me to overtask my strength.

"No, — but I have read enough, perhaps, for this morning."

I mounted the ladder to my room, and occupied myself until summoned to dinner. Edward was present, but it was not the hour for conversation. No allusion was made by my hostess to the topics of the morning. Edward spoke gayly of his occupations without, and seemed eager to return to them. His eyes turned more than once to the window during the brief meal. It was his German aid who was watched for. No sooner did his square bulk loom up in the distance than Edward rose and left us with a few hasty words of excuse.

At supper — the longest and most important of our meals — the farmer was once more the attentive and agreeable host. He thanked me cordially for the pleasure I had given his mother. I soon perceived that her confidences had extended farther. A slight agitation, discernible through the habitual calm of his manner, betrayed that to the rustic poet himself, as well as to his mother, the hour was a serious one which was to initiate a stranger into the most sacred of their household mysteries.

As soon as supper was over, I approached without circumlocution the subject which I knew was in all our thoughts, and boldly asked Edward to furnish from his own stores the entertainment of the evening. He assented frankly, and, going to a case of shelves attached to the wall, took from it several portfolios. He turned his eyes towards his mother and stood as if waiting for her to decide his choice.

"Read first —— no, begin with the 'Tragedy of Errors.'"

He selected one of the portfolios, and, seating himself near me, laid it upon the table before him.

"A drama?" I asked.

"It is in the dramatic form, but not intended for the stage."

He opened his portfolio, but remained silent, as if collecting confidence to begin. I availed myself of this pause to tell him that he must not overrate my critical skill; that I had too little to be dreaded, or even to be very useful; in giving my opinion of a literary work, I pretended to know only what interested or moved me.

"I shall be satisfied, if I interest you; more than satisfied, if I move you. If I fail to do either, you will tell me so frankly, and not let me make myself tedious?"

I promised, and quite sincerely.

Before beginning to read, Edward announced the dramatis personæ, and gave me some particulars in regard to them and to the scene of his drama. While thus introducing his personages, and afterwards when discussing them with me, he spoke of them rather as of persons whom he had familiarly known than as of creations of his fancy. He seemed to regard some of them with a sympathy quite real, others with a dislike equally sincere. He mentioned occurrences in the lives of some of them which I did not find in the play, and gave fuller details in regard to incidents introduced into it. From these circumstances I inferred that some at least of his characters were drawn from the life, and that the narrative itself had a groundwork of truth.

The scene of the "Tragedy of Errors" is laid on a beautiful plantation, which Colvil described to me as if his walks and rides had often lain through it. The time is not distinctly defined, but it is in the nineteenth century, and, as I inferred from some passages in it, prior to 1830. The action of the piece is comprised within the limits of a single day. It is not divided into acts, but into five parts: Morning, Noon, Afternoon, Evening, Night.

"Morning" opens in a wide glade, in which the field-hands and the other slaves of the plantation are assembled to celebrate a joyful festival. Two days of unrestrained liberty have been granted by their wealthy and indulgent master, and these they prepare to crowd with every enjoyment which their condition leaves open to them. Detached groups gather on the wide plain, — some dancing, others singing in chorus, others engaged in athletic games. The foreground is occupied by the higher order of slaves. Minstrels and preachers succeed one another. Emotions, glad, mournful, and solemn, pass in turn over the impressible crowd.

This scene serves as a sort of prologue, in which are sketched out the antecedents and the surroundings of the personages about to be introduced. A few figures detach themselves from the shifting groups that glide by to disappear, and connect themselves in the imagination with the action of the opening drama. The scene is one of unrestrained freedom and diversion. The actors in it, beings without responsibility or forecast, should enjoy without that alloy of regrets and apprehensions which intrudes on the brief season allowed to pleasure by the thoughtful and self-denying freeman. But neither absolute power nor absolute dependence exempts man from his inheritance of care. The pale cheek of woe and the lowering brow of hate find room among these smiling faces. Through the tones of the careless melody and the pious prayer, the ear detects a latent discord and a smothered curse.

The tragedy begins with a festival. It unfolds in the midst of ease and security. Belrespiro is the abode of wealth and refinement. But the luxurious modern mansion, with its prosaic comforts and elegances, may, as the theatre of human passions, not less than the Pelasgic palace or the mediæval fortress, attain to all the dignities of crime and sorrow. The second scene of Morning introduces us into a room in the house at Belrespiro. It is simply furnished, — its chief decoration consisting of natural flowers. The windows, opening upon a long portico, are partially shaded by the festoons of luxuriant vines. Three persons are present. The most striking figure is a man of middle age, seated near the window. It is Stanley, the master of the house. He attracts by his handsome person, and by a certain easy grace of manner. Stanley is an accomplished, highly-bred man of the world, — polite to his wife, hospitable to his neighbors, indulgent to his servants. He has one profound affection, — that which he bears his beautiful daughter. To her he gives a respect which his experience of life permits him to accord but seldom.

Near Mr. Stanley is seated a short, square-built man, with white hair worn long and falling carelessly about a broad, frank, meditative face. It is Doctor Hermann, a German refugee, formerly tutor of the daughter of the house.

On a sofa in the middle of the room, Emma Fortescue, the wife of Stanley, reclines listlessly. Her delicate fingers play with a spray of cluster-roses. From time to time she turns her languid eyes towards the window. She has the beauty of refinement, of grace, of taste. In her toilet, and in the arrangements of this her favorite room, the simplest means produce charming effects. Her voice is plaintive, with at times a touch of the querulousness of the invalid; but when she is deeply moved, it is low and pathetic. Her life has two pleasures, — music and flowers. Emma was born in a tropical climate. Her father, an American planter, had married a rich West-Indian widow, who died in giving her birth. Emma was consigned to the charge of a married sister almost twenty years older than herself, who lavished upon her the same tenderness she bestowed on her own child, a little girl of the same age. When Emma was seven years old, her father claimed her, and took her with him to the United States. The little West-Indian had not ceased to grieve for her first home when a new calamity befell her, from whose depressing effects she never completely recovered. Her beloved sister, with her husband and children, was on her way to the United States. They were already expected at the house of Mr. Fortescue, when, in their stead, arrived the news of the wreck of the vessel in which they had sailed and the probable loss of all the passengers. Nothing was learned of the fate of Emma's relatives. It was never known whether they were of those who remained with the sinking ship and found a speedy death beneath the waves, or of those who secured for themselves a place on one of the hastily constructed rafts and suffered a more protracted agony. The storm which wrecked them had been of such violence that it had reached far inland; the child had herself trembled, as she looked from the window and saw the devastation around her and heard the crashing of the pines not far from her father's house. Emma Fortescue was then ten years old. From that time she led a vacant life until her marriage. The man whom her father presented to her as her husband was full of attentions to his bride, and never ceased to bestow on his wife every indulgence that wealth could furnish. If with this complaisance was mingled a shade of contempt, the consciousness was confined closely to his own breast. The husband and wife live side by side, but in different worlds. He does not surmise that the apathetic existence which flows on indolently near his own covers an under-life of revolt and passion.

Some of those vague portents that attract, perhaps, for a moment, the mystical mind, but are commonly slighted by those whom they should warn, offer themselves to the little party at Belrespiro, met to await the arrival of the absent daughter and heiress. In the soft twilight of the shaded room, as in the sunshine of the open glade, hovers the shadow of an approaching Nemesis.

Such are the impressions I retain of the first evening's reading. With my recollections of the play itself I have doubtless mingled some of Colvil's comments and explanations,—sometimes, perhaps, even retaining his own words.

I had then the habit of keeping a journal. I gave it up when I was married, and have not since resumed it. But, at that period, I found great satisfaction in intrusting my thoughts and experiences to this silent confidant,—silent for all the rest of the world, eloquent for me. My present adventure—for such my young imagination did not hesitate to call the arrival and detention at a lonely farm-house—had already filled some pages, intended to recall, at a future time, in all its vividness, the story of that happy week; this evening furnished several more. All else that was present to me then has disappeared: youth, friendship, confidence. A second life, with other interests and other hopes, has intervened, and has vanished in its turn. Little record, you are faithful to your office; yet the man to whom you deliver up your secrets is not the same who confided them to you.

III.

THE next morning the sun shone out brightly, the air was fresh. I hailed the prospect of freedom with the delight of a convalescent. Yet I apprehended some maternal objections on the part of my anxious hostess. When I came down, I found that a council had already been held over me, and my enlargement decreed. Edward proposed that I should accompany him to the scene of his labors, but immediately bethought himself and withdrew his invitation: I was not yet strong enough; I must keep on the higher land; the ground to which his work called him was low and damp. I began to remonstrate; but Mrs. Colvil seconded her son's objection, and even Tabitha put in her protest: I was not going off to leave the breakfast she had ready for me? I would not admit that my health was not sufficiently restored to enable me to brave any danger which my friend could encounter, but, finding it was in vain for me to withstand the united forces of the family, I surrendered to Tabitha, who led the way in triumph to the breakfast-table.

When I had praised her skill both by word and deed, I selected from the shelves a few books to be the companions of my walk; for I knew beforehand that the landscape would furnish few suggestions to the fancy. Indeed, the only variety it offered was in the shifting forms of the clouds, and the occasional obscurity which they cast over the scene, and which was more consonant with its monotony than the blazing sunshine which it momentarily displaced. No flicker of light and shade about me, no blue hills in the distance. In one direction, I could trace, by their slight, broken fringe, the low banks of the slowly moving river which blessed and threatened the neighborhood; in another, a pine-wood bounded my view with a black line.

I walked to a considerable distance from the house before I found a tree that threw a shadow broad enough for me to rest in. At last I stopped near a forlorn pine that had survived its tribe, and seated myself on the blackened stump of one of its fallen companions. I threw my books on the grass; for, after all, I did not need them. The melancholy of the scene acted on my imagination as pleasantly as the richest and most varied landscape could have done. I fell into day-dreams, charming, but tranquil. The misty world of the future rolled out before me. From the point where

I was, branched out many paths, all equally attractive. I entered one of them, followed it for a time, then left it suddenly for another, which I gave up abruptly in its turn, to take one that seemed for the moment more alluring, or its end more worthy to be sought. But in whatever direction Fancy led me, whether she lured me by visions of ambition, of romance, of daring enterprise, in all her pictures the image of my new friend was constant. In every effort, in every success, he was by my side as partaker or as confidant. Again, I abdicated my heroship in his favor, and made him the principal in the scenes in which I now consented in my turn to bear the secondary part. This part was not without its dignity. It was I who was to furnish to the humble poet the courage and resolution through which his now obscure work was to become fruitful to other minds than his own. I was to take on myself the practical, the material part. He was to know nothing of these irksome details. He was only to enjoy the success and be encouraged by it to higher efforts. In the end there was for him emancipation from this narrow life, and in its place ease, fame; for his mother, the reward of her exertions and faith; for me, the joys of disinterested friendship, and perhaps something of the generous pride of the artificer of another's fortune.

When I had reached this climax, I returned to

earth to examine a little more closely the groundwork on which my castle had been raised. I called up the scenes which had passed before me the last evening. I revived the impression they had made upon me, and soon lost myself in them as completely as in my own dreams. As I thus stood among the dark groups in the glade at Belrespiro, looking into the smiling or brooding faces, and listening to the light or mournful songs, a flood of rich melody was poured upon the air, leaving me for a moment in doubt whether it were of my dream or of the outer world. As I collected myself to listen, it had ceased. After a few moments the same strain was repeated, and again after another interval, like the song of a bird, and it seemed to gush from a like fountain of inward delight. I rose, and, turning, saw the erect form of Tabitha moving in the direction of the house. Her arms were folded. She bore on her head a large basket. She went with a slow, measured step. It was plain that she was about no task that was to be got through with to make way for another or for rest, but that she was engaged in the serious performance of an office of which she felt all the dignity. I asked myself, as I had already asked myself more than once before, — Was this simplicity a thing to be admired or looked down upon?

This interruption did not change the current of my thoughts, but gave them a more definite object. I began to compare the imaginary sketches with the reality. I passed in review the examples of this foreign race which had come under my notice, and sought for the poetical element which might lie obscured for me by the double veil of my prejudice and their unconsciousness. I had already begun, before I saw Colvil, to feel an increasing interest in this dark people, so bound up with us and so separated from us, always aliens in our eyes, but in their own as much children of the soil as ourselves.

I had learned, while I had been travelling in the Southern country, that the feeling which prevailed there towards this race differed much from that then entertained in the North. I found that the contempt felt for the negro by the Southerner is not founded on antipathy to the race, but attaches to the condition of slave, the idea of which is associated with his color. In the North, on the contrary, where negroes are comparatively rare, and where the white man is seldom brought into intimate relations with them, the pity which this condition inspires is kept in check by a certain reluctance to salute as a brother a being secretly suspected of usurping the form of humanity without a capacity for its nobler manifestations. I had brought with me to the South something of this feeling, but it had been gradually undergoing modification. I speedily became dispossessed of the notion that any natural antipathy exists between the two races, and began even to doubt whether the natural inequality were so great as I had taken for granted it must be. I had observed that not only does the Southern infant cling as closely to its negro nurse as the Northern infant to its Irish one, but that the older children, in families in which the relation of master and slave was on a kindly footing, looked up to their attendant with confiding affection, and received her counsels with even more respect than the admonitions of a Northern nursery-maid are apt to meet with from her charge. I had seen that the pillow of the sick was smoothed as acceptably by a dark hand as by a fair one. I had seen that in the family-council the old servant had a voice, and often a decisive one. In fine, I saw, that, in spite of all the hindrances interposed by a servile condition and its concomitants, the dark members of a Southern family not infrequently obtained that ascendancy which is acquired only by superiority in character and intellect.

When I was myself brought into closer contact with the descendant of the African, I found, almost with surprise, that his modes of thought were not so strange to me, that his feelings were not outside the pale of my sympathies, and that the expression of them was often such as I might have adopted without discredit. The image of the traditional Sambo which I had brought with me was displaced by one more like the reality. It is true, that, in the work-field, and in the coffle, on its forced migrations, I had more than once encountered grotesque specimens of the race; but I was aware that here influences had been at work which no form of humanity can resist, and that the by-streets of European cities could offer examples of as low a type. I did not, therefore, generalize from these. I knew, indeed, that, in the opinion of experts in these matters, the negro was never destined to shine in metaphysics or in mathematics. Perhaps it was because I had not yet discovered in myself any special aptitude for either of these sciences, that I did not feel myself bound to disclaim relationship with him on that ground. As my opportunities for information enlarged, I became convinced, both by my own observation and from stories told me by Southern planters, that, in the noblest attributes of humanity, in sense of justice, in benevolence, in magnanimity, the dark man had fully established his claims to brotherhood with our best.

In aid of my gradual enlightenment, came back a reminiscence of my childhood. Among its shadowy images moved the form of a black man. But this man always stood for me separated from his race. He had a foreign air and accent. He seemed to me more like a figure out of an Eastern tale than like a vulgar negro. I had heard wonderful stories of him, as the guardian of a beautiful lady, as the unseen benefactor of noble exiles. He was for me a man mysterious and apart. When I learned his condition and history more accurately, they took a more prosaic character. Still I had never classed him with the common negro, nor thought of drawing from his virtues conclusions favorable to the race. But the proofs which had recently come to my knowledge of the height of excellence to which the negro character was capable of attaining had made me ask myself more than once whether the marvel of my childhood was not perhaps a perfect example rather than an exception.

Some vestiges of a prejudice remain, even after the reason has been disabused. It was thus in my case. I believed that I had arrived at a state of entire candor in my judgment of the black man, but in my relations with him I was still conscious of a sense of distance greater than that which separated me from the white man of humble rank. I had observed that the mind of Colvil was much more free from such prepossessions than my own. He had neither the antipathy of a Northerner for an alien race, nor the contempt of a Southerner for an abject one. I thought I could perceive that his prevailing sentiment towards this unfortunate people was one of not disrespectful compassion. The scenes which he had brought before me had heightened the interest I had begun to feel in this race and my desire to form a more correct estimate of its genius and character.

These scenes still occupied my fancy when I met him at dinner. I was eager to pour out upon him the ideas they had set in movement. When I had several times returned to my topic after the conversation had diverged from it, he perceived that I wished to draw him into a discussion. He did not decline it. When our simple meal was concluded, instead of leaving me, as I had feared, he lingered, as if held by the attraction of the subject; yet uneasily in the beginning, — for he knew, and so did I, that the broad German was on the look-out for him somewhere; but, at last, after a questioning glance at the landscape without, as if taking counsel in some case of conflicting duties, he seemed to decide the matter within himself, and, happily, in my favor.

He spoke like a man who does not deliberately intrude on another a subject which lies near his own heart, but who enters upon it gladly when he sees the promise of a sincere interest. He spoke with feeling, yet with a certain restraint, as if afraid of endangering my sympathy by overtaxing it.

He called my attention to the fact that the dark men of America form a new race, and can no longer, with any propriety, be called African. He made me remark, too, that they are a very mixed race, and, as such, entitled, at a future time, to contribute some vigorous passages to the story of humanity.

"The blood," he said, "of the conquering Felatah, of the enduring Muzgu, of the song-loving Sulima, of the ingenious Mandingo, of the intrepid Begharmi, mingles in the veins of this rising people with that of some of the highest European races. Here and there we indeed find, in some individual, the original type of one of these contributing tribes or nations reproduced in its purity. The slave-trader's favorite booty, the Macqua, is found as ugly and as hardy on the banks of some of our rivers as on those of the Zambesi; I have seen wild dances which it seemed only the transmigrated soul of a Nijempani could have animated; you gave, and aptly, the name of 'Spanish Don' to the major-domo at the Highlands; there is a sturdy Saxon at the anvil not twenty miles from us; and I have seen in the cotton-field unmistakable Celts. But, notwithstanding the marked contrasts offered by individuals, this new people is gradually assuming characteristics which we recognize as general. In conversing with persons of this race, we are sensible of a certain originality in their views. Their humor, their pathos, has a different quality from that of the Anglo-Saxon; their thought has another shading than ours.

"It has seemed to me that this element, so foreign, yet so familiar to me, is to be recognized in Alexander Dumas. I think I feel the African soul in his exuberant genius, which moves along with such a careless delight in itself,—in the irresistible drollery that laughs and mocks through his pages,—in his light satire, so piquant, yet so woundless. Perhaps the African descent that is claimed for the Russian poet Puschkin may be thought to reveal itself in the luxuriant growth of his imagery, in the soft fall of his verse, which flows, one of his countrymen says, 'like pearls over velvet.'

"The dark men of America are not, more than any other people, to be judged by their lowest class. When we speak of the English, we do not mean the pale masses of the manufacturing towns, nor the troglodyte population of the coal regions. No more, when we would judge of the capacities of our dark countrymen, should we consider them in the resentful or apathetic renderers of a forced domestic service, nor in the imbruted gangs of the rice-plantation.

"I was much struck by the account of the moral condition of Europeans who had been held in slavery by the Arabs, given by Mr. Dupuis, who was British Vice-Consul in Mogadore at a time when white Christians still stood on equal terms with black Pagans in the Barbary slave-markets, and when the crews of vessels wrecked on the Sahara coast were a lawful prize. Mr. Dupuis was instrumental in obtaining the release of many of these unfortunate men. He says, that, 'on their first arrival in Mogadore, those that have been any considerable time in slavery appear lost to reason and feeling,' — that they are 'indifferent to everything, abject, servile, and brutified,' — that 'their spirits are broken, their faculties sunk in stupor.' 'It seems,' he says, 'that the hardships they have endured, without any protecting law to which they can apply for redress, have destroyed every spring of exertion or hope.' And he saw them only after their release! It is not surprising that the Arab of Africa felt contempt for Europeans and Christians, since he probably formed his opinion from those he had known as his own slaves. Is not as rash a judgment sometimes pronounced on the bondmen of America?

"It has been my fortune to study them on the estate of a wealthy and indulgent master, a man of refined tastes, to whom deliberate cruelty would have been abhorrent, and who was both too proud and too fond of ease to exact of his dependents more than they cheerfully rendered. The new-comer there might have been received with the consolation which Clytemnestra offered to Cassandra :—

> 'It is no wrathful Fate that sends thee hither,
> To take thy place among our many slaves.
> Since bondage was decreed thee, great the boon
> To serve a house of long-established wealth;
> For those whom chance has suddenly enriched
> Are hard in all things, and observe no measure.
> Here thou wilt have that which is suitable.'

"Every privilege, indeed, which custom has anywhere secured to the slave was, on this plantation, accorded as a right. The hours of work were reasonable, food abundant, holidays not infrequent. A certain amount of service performed, the workman owned his time and his strength. He might spend them on labor of his choice, or squander them on leisure. The slaves on this plantation did not live under that systematic subjection, that iron routine, which deadens the higher nature as fatally as a rougher tyranny crushes it. They were permitted to be men. With them, affection was not without sentiment, nor passion without dignity. The soul, not wholly the prisoner and servant of the body, announced its own separate wants, and sought and found their satisfaction.

The life of these dependent people had its shades certainly, and deep ones, but even these were not unfavorable to the development of the poetic and religious faculties.

"On this plantation I have frequently mingled with the light-hearted crowd on days of festival, or with the same crowd transformed into devout worshippers on occasions of religious solemnity. They came to disregard my presence, and were no more constrained before me than with each other. I have often stood in sincere admiration before their minstrels, and still oftener before their preachers."

"But do not the inaccuracies of their language and the imperfections of their pronunciation detract from the effect of their eloquence?"

"The men of real ability among them seldom speak inaccurately, — that is, illogically; and true eloquence overbears all minor defects."

"Yet sometimes," I replied, "at our own political meetings, when listening to a man of real power, but deficient culture, I have found the effect not merely of his eloquence, but almost of his arguments, lost upon me."

"There are certain modes of expression, and, above all, certain intonations, to which we attach the idea of vulgarity; and this association is often too strong for our judgment. I know something of this weakness, myself. My father was a purist in language. He was strict in the repression of innovation. His ear was almost over-sensitive in regard to defective modulation and slovenly enunciation, which, it must be allowed, offend too often in our public speakers. My linguistic pursuits have made me very catholic in regard to forms of speech; diversities in these interest me as varieties of a plant a botanist; but I have still something of my father's sensibility to tones and inflections,—which, indeed, are influenced by something deeper than fashion or habit."

"I have observed," I said, "that the higher class of this dark race have pleasant voices, and modulate them agreeably. In truth, I have sometimes found them superior in this respect to those they served."

"They have a sense of beauty and harmony, which expresses itself whenever and however their condition permits."

"I have heard much," I said, after a few moments' pause, "of the eloquence of African preachers, but I have not yet had the good-fortune to meet with one who justified their reputation."

"It is possible you may not have it. It has more than once been my chance to observe a remarkable phenomenon. I have been standing entranced, like the rest of his hearers, before one of these rude prophets, when suddenly the electric current has been broken. The spell by which he held his audience is dissolved. The seer has vanished. An ordinary man is before you, dealing out commonplaces in language trite or turgid. I have looked for the explanation, — nor long. A party of white persons had entered, — fashionable women, perhaps, and men condescending or supercilious, — brought by curiosity to hear a specimen of negro eloquence."

"The poor slave! even in his moments of exaltation, he is quelled by the lordly eye of his superior."

"I believe," replied Edward, "that, in general, it is not awe that works the change, but the sudden introduction of an unsympathizing element."

"I have seen the same failure in an illiterate white preacher of real eloquence, when called to speak before a cultivated audience. I confess, in his case, I thought the desire of being equal to his reputation had something to do with his falling so far below it. He abandoned his usual simple, nervous language for a studied diction, and made a little display of scholarship quite uncalled-for. I afterwards heard him in his own Bethel, and formed a very different estimate of his powers."

"Among the weaker sort," Edward answered, "vanity has, no doubt, a share in this sudden destitution of apostolic gifts. I have seen among the black preachers men of real ability, sincere men, too, make themselves absurd, when called upon to speak before an audience composed of white persons. This is especially apt to be the case when the occasion has been foreseen and prepared for. But, in general, this temporary suspension or inthralment of the powers, of which we have been speaking, is due neither to servility nor self-love, but to an influence of which all men are more or less susceptible. No faculty is more under the control of exhilarating or depressing influences than that of language. Sympathy is the breath of life to the poet. I have known men strong enough to hold themselves independent of it, — yet few. These have been men severely schooled by suffering, and whose whole being was possessed by an earnest purpose. The slave does not commonly want the needed discipline; and when he is great enough to be formed, not crushed by it, no man is more likely to devote himself to a single and unselfish object. The adoration of the Deity, and the awakening of other souls to His love and worship, often make the voluntary life of the man whose material existence has no office for his will or his hope."

"I can understand the power of these men over their fellows, but not that they should have any over you. Yet it is true that those who are in continual attendance on their masters wear off all coarseness, and have nothing in their manner which offends."

"The ablest and most eloquent among them," said Edward, smiling, "are not usually those who are in constant communication with the master race, nor, indeed, those who have received most instruction. They are more commonly found among the followers of mechanic arts which employ the hands without engrossing the thoughts. These men enjoy greater independence than the others. They are necessarily more trusted to themselves. They are forced to use their own faculties. They do not commonly work under the eye of a task-master. They are not obliged to be always ready at call. Wood-cutting, cattle-tending, boating of produce, any occupation which implies a certain independence and gives opportunity for silent meditation, is more favorable than household service. Agriculture on a small plantation, where few hands are employed, does not so much impede the expansion of the intellect. But the obsequiousness, the alertness, required of a domestic servant, accord very ill with the grand, tranquil flow of religious inspiration. And the wretch — one of a gang as abject as himself — who has toiled all day under the lash of a driver, what has he strength for but perhaps a dumb, imploring prayer to a Protection divined, but not yet made manifest?"

"But from what source do the men you speak of draw their ideas, their language?"

"They owe, indeed," Edward answered, "little to schools. And that great garden of modern literature in which we wander at will, passing from one flower or fruit to another so carelessly that we hardly know well the perfume or flavor of any, is shut to them. But they have, perhaps, their compensation. If they are confined to one volume, it is a volume which is in itself a library. Let us not forget that they have been trained by that great teacher through whose influence England learned to speak with one tongue and to feel with one heart, — the same that gave to Germany a classic language, and that infused into the springing literature of these countries those elements of elevation and energy that have distinguished the productions of English and German mind from those of any other modern people. Shall we call that man uncultivated whose mind is imbued with the deep wisdom, the sublime devotion, the grand imagery of the Book of Books? And where shall we find a better school of language, a deeper well of English undefiled, than in our common version of the Old and New Testaments?"

"Do all these preachers know how to read?"

"Many of them. Those who do not, when they are men of strong intellect, lose less by the deprivation than we are apt to suppose. For every aid that civilization gives us, we sacrifice something of our self-reliance, and, with this, something of our power. The force of memory possessed by some of these men, who cannot store learning up in libraries and find it ready to their hand, but must trust to their own brain for the preservation of whatever mental treasures they collect, would astonish many a German scholar. Only the Druids, perhaps, may have surpassed them. Their wealth, too, is gathered slowly; each new accession is pondered and scrutinized."

"I have had few opportunities of listening to negro eloquence. I once, indeed, heard a black man relate to an audience of his own race a mournful incident in simple and touching language. I was moved with the rest. But when he heightened the pathos of his narrative by noting the fineness of the handkerchief with which his heroine dried her tears, my sympathies received a sudden shock. He passed from the grief of the bereaved to the procession of carriages to the grave, and described with unction the splendor and profusion of the funeral-feast. I have always found my interest thus cut short. It is true, I have heard no black preacher of eminence. I have seen reports of negro discourses in which I have found originality certainly, and rude power; but the grotesque and vulgar images, which no doubt were well enough adapted to those they were meant for, would, I am afraid, have made me laugh in spite of myself, if I had been of the audience."

"Perhaps we should have found ourselves laughing, if, with our modern ideas, we could have heard Homer reciting the retreat of Ajax, whom he compares to an ass belabored by boys, who break their sticks on his sluggish back, and hardly get him out of the corn-field when he has eaten himself full. And what shall we say of his comparing a hero tossing on his bed, revolving his griefs and projects of vengeance, to a hungry man hastily turning and re-turning his dinner on the coals, impatient to see it cooked? This would be found a very droll simile, if we heard it used by a negro on a pathetic occasion.

"Homer's unconsciousness of the scale of dignities established by modern taste has been a sore trial to his translators. It is hard upon them, with their refined notions, to oblige them to compare warriors pressing out to battle to wasps irritated by mischievous boys,—men following their leader to the fight to sheep following the ram to water,—a hero walking distractedly about the body of his fallen companion to a cow moving round and round her first calf. We have little conception of the sort of equality that exists between man and the other animals, where they live familiarly together, as in primitive life, ancient or modern. We hardly understand comparing a man to a beast at all, unless in derision; at least, it must be to a wild one, who is to us almost a fabulous being.

"It is not easy to render in language dignified enough for modern ears the cooking scene in which Achilles cuts up the meat and Patroclus tends it roasting. In those old times, the physical had, if not a greater, a more recognized importance than now. Food, clothing, as essential to man, nor yet altogether a matter of course, were entitled to respectful mention. Nestor, when he tries to incite one of the chiefs to go out to reconnoitre the Trojans, promises him, in the first place, boundless glory, and then that he shall be invited to all the feasts. Zeus himself is touched, when he sees Achilles fasting while the rest of the chiefs are at the banquet. The relenting Achilles invites the suppliant Priam to dine, reminding him that even the beautiful-haired Niobe remembered food when fatigued with weeping. Priam not declining, the swift Achilles kills a sheep; his companions skin it, cut it up, spit the pieces, and roast them judiciously. All being ready, Automedon hands the bread, but Achilles himself helps to the meat. When Andromache, in her first anguish after the death of Hector, forebodes the fate of her little son, she sees him, who used to 'eat marrow on his father's lap,' sipping from a charitable cup enough to wet his lips, but not to quench his thirst, and walking timidly near the table where his father's equals sit with their sons, looking for a place where he can crowd in.

"Dress is a matter of moment with Homer. He has pleasure in embroidered mantles, in soft woollen vestments, in bright red belts, in handsome sandals. When his heroes prepare to go forth, their toilet is described, — the more minutely, the greater the personage. When Agamemnon wakes from his false dream, eager to take Troy that very day, the soft tunic which he puts on, beautiful and new, the great cloak, the handsome shoes he binds on his glossy feet, are of too much importance to be passed over in silence, whatever the haste to summon the assembly. The poet would increase our respect for Andromache by telling us she is attended by a well-dressed maid. When this princess falls backward senseless, he does not omit to tell us that her beautiful head-dress drops off; he delays a moment to describe it, and tq tell us how she came by her veil. Telemachus, when he takes off at night his soft garment, gives it to his old nurse, who folds it carefully and hangs it on a peg. Ulysses describes minutely his cloak with its embroidery and its golden clasp, and the tunic, supple and shining, which sat on him 'as the skin on a dried onion.' 'Many women,' he says, 'gazed upon it.' The goddesses themselves are supposed to have a taste in dress. Even the venerable daughter of Kronos cannot dispense with embroidery and golden clasps. She must have a hundred tassels to her girdle, nor is the tip jewel enough for the 'well-bored' celestial ear.

"The primitive poets have no artificial standard of dignity. They have that simple self-respect which makes a man feel that whatever really impresses or interests him is worthy to do so.

"If you were to listen to one of these field-preachers of whom I speak, you would find in their discourses a truly sublime thought, a tender touch of Nature, immediately followed by what would seem to you an incongruity or a bathos. You would find things of very unequal interest, in your eyes, put on the same level. When we would judge of these men, who, through their condition, are at a distance of ages from our peculiar civilization, we must make the same allowances that we do in the case of the ancients. I am persuaded that those illustrations and descriptions which the critics cavil at in Homer and the other poets of antiquity would seem natural and striking to one of them.

"I once saw a lady, who deigned to listen to a negro preacher, highly amused when he quoted the text, 'Woe unto them that draw iniquity with cords of vanity, and sin as it were with a cart-rope!' She kindly dropped her veil to hide her merriment, when, shortly after, she heard him say, — 'For the bed is shorter than that a man can stretch himself on it, and the covering narrower than that he can wrap himself in it.' She supposed he was drawing his homely illustrations from his own customary occupations and accommodations, and did not surmise that her mirth was moved, not by the negro Isaiah, but by the greatest of the Hebrew prophets. These metaphors might have been the preacher's own. He adopted them, no doubt, because he had a full sense of their force. But he had an equal sense of the force of imagery drawn from the grandest objects in Nature, for he had lived among them. The hills, the clouds, the winds, the rushing torrents, had been his companions; he found his illustrations in them, in the implements of his labor, in the surroundings of his actual life, indifferently.

"These new men have the courage which belongs to the writers and orators of youthful peoples. They have not the fear of critics before their eyes. They trust to their own intuitive sense of the force of words, and draw their images from objects familiar to themselves and their hearers. We moderns — the educated and half-educated of us, above all — are so afraid to rely upon ourselves, that even for our metaphors we want an authority. It would almost seem that they are the more readily adopted, the less we are qualified to judge of their propriety. We talk of *lynx-eyed*, though most of us know nothing of the eye-sight of the lynx except from hearsay. 'A fox in cunning,' 'A lion in courage,' are familiar phrases in the mouths of people who have not had experience of the qualities of these animals, and who, if they had, would perhaps find their names less to the purpose. I believe that those who know the lion well find him a vulgar animal. I dare say in Africa a 'lion-hearted king' would mean a king with a heart like his of Dahomey.

"So pedantic are we, that a too bold simile or an out-of-the-way word can blind us to a good thought and take the charm from pathos. What should we say to these lines, if they were written now?

> 'But when she felt
> Herself down soust, she wakèd out of dread
> Straight into grief.'

Or these?

> 'Seven months he so her kept in bitter smart,
> Until such time as noble Britomart
> Releasèd her that else was like to starve
> Through cruel knife that her dear heart did carve.'

"We are obliged to put up with the old poets; but let a word which has become strange, or is employed now only in a trivial sense, be used as they would have used it, and we are offended or childishly amused.

"I am not taking the part of eccentricity. A man who understands these conventionalities and advisedly shocks them is as far from the simplicity which alone gives force and dignity as the uncultivated man who attempts a phraseology finer than is natural to him. What I mean to say is, that we are disqualified by this fastidiousness for judging of men who have not been trained in the same fashions and prejudices. We find them ridiculous because their expressions are so to our ears. There are those to whom, by traditional use, certain words, to us obsolete, have the same force they had to Spenser. We misjudge men of our own race, of a different cultivation; how much more the blacks, who have still less opportunity of learning the fashionable use of words!

"'But to his speech he answerèd no whit,
But stood still mute, as if he had been dum,
Ne sign of sense did show, ne common wit,
As one with griefe and anguish overcum,
And unto everything did answer mum.'

"If this were brought forward as a specimen of negro verse, I believe it would excite no little merriment; but imagine the respectful change of countenance, when it should be announced that it belongs to him

> 'Whose deep conceit is such
> As passing all conceit needs no defence.'

"If we come to the peculiarities of the negro pronunciation, — peculiarities rapidly wearing out with the higher class of blacks, — why should we find in the inability or neglect of this recently foreign race to pronounce our language as we do something absurd and comic, and regard it as a sign of inferiority? The differences between their pronunciation and ours are of the same nature with those which distinguished the various dialects which flowed together to form our mother-tongue, — of the same nature with those that are found at the present day in the pronunciation of the same word by different nations of the Gothic stock. If our dark countryman, in offering the prayer, which he sends up with more fervor and perhaps with more real faith than most of us do, 'Give us this day our daily bread,' says *gib* where we say *give*, he pronounces this word no otherwise than Luther did; if he calls father *fader*, so did the great Swede, the champion of Protestant Christendom. In our own language, we have, in more than one case, authority for two forms of the same word. Do we venture to smile at Milton when he calls a leopard a *libbard?*

> 'The libbard, and the tiger, and the mole,
> Rising, the crumbled earth above them threw.'

Spenser tells us that the river Se*v*ern takes its name from the fair Sa*b*rina; and that 'De*b*ons shaire was, that is De*v*onshire.' We take a pleasure in tracing these mutations and divergences, where our equals in blood are concerned; it is only in the case of the Africo-American that they become matter of derision. Yet he has often only gone forward in the path our ancestors travelled before him, and yet more often unconsciously retraced it. When he says *I hab* for *I have*, he goes back to the Anglo-Saxon, (*habbe*,) coincides with the ancient Roman (*habeo*) and with the modern German (*habe*). The negro would understand more readily than we the motto,—

Lybba þú þæt þú lybbe.

"If we come to real mutilations of the language, we shall find we keep him in countenance better than we allow. We smile when he calls his mistress his *missis;* but the dignified *magistressa*, having been first reduced to *mistress*, has suffered this further degradation with us too, though we disguise it from ourselves by writing the word in this case with three letters, *Mrs.*, one of which is no longer heard in it. We write it phonetically, when we would represent negro-talk."

All this time we had remained sitting at the

table. Tabitha had for some minutes been hovering near it with a disturbed and uncertain expression, whose meaning I well understood, though I was careful not to betray my recognition of it. She cast, from time to time, an inquiring glance at her mistress, who did not respond, her eyes being intent on her work, and her mind, apparently, upon our conversation. Poor Tabitha's look grew constantly more imploring and her movements more significant, until they at last drew the attention of Edward, who, with a kind smile and a motion of his hand, gave her the permission she was waiting for. She instantly bore down upon the table and began the removal of the dinner-equipage, whose neglect had been long reproaching her punctual conscience. With true African tact, however, she performed her task with as much celerity and as little noise as possible. I had expected to see her, as usual, plant her kettle of steaming water in the midst of the great hearth and assemble all her plates and dishes about it, in order to perform her after-dinner functions with all due state and ceremony. I reproached myself for a slight sense of irritation I had felt in advance, when I saw the considerate creature carrying all this apparatus out of the house, with the evident intention of accomplishing these solemn rites in the open air. The animated clash which always signalled their performance thus came softened to our ears, and made an apt accompaniment to the song which was a necessary part of the ceremonial. This song, in which the plaintive and the merry were quaintly mingled, harmonized with the thoughts our conversation had called up. As it now rose in wild, jubilant strains, now sank to an almost inaudible sigh, it seemed as if the good and evil genius of Africa were at watch, alternately revelling and grieving near us.

We sat for a few moments in silence. The song died away to a monotonous chant. It was as if the struggle and the hope were over, and the old torpor had settled down again.

IV.

"You are beginning," said Edward, the next morning, when he found himself held at the breakfast-table by the questions I had in store for him, suggested by the conversation of the day before, — "you are beginning to come under the influence of the charm which this tropic race, in whose nature and lot the pathetic and the humorous are so strangely mingled, exerts over a Northern imagination."

"You have felt it?"

"I felt it as you do, when I first came in contact with them. But this attraction, blended of surprise and pity, gradually gave place to a deeper sentiment, as I knew them better and reflected more seriously on their condition."

"I believe I should feel an affection for them, if I saw much of them; though perhaps you are right in supposing that as yet it is my imagination that is interested, rather than my heart. I think I should make a study of their character, as you have, if I stayed long among them. It often puzzles me. I fall sometimes from admiration to contempt, in a way that is unpleasant. I was a short time ago at the house of a planter whose embarrassments had forced him to sell some of his slaves, — among others, one who had served him in a responsible place with ability and integrity. My host was kind-hearted, and felt this necessity deeply, especially in the case of this particular man. But he owned to me that his regrets were somewhat relieved, when he found that the poor fellow, in the midst of his grief, had room for resentment at the low price for which he had been sold, which he regarded as an indignity. I had felt so much sympathy for the man, that I was angry with him and myself, when, against my will, I found myself smiling at this absurdity."

"And yet a similar pride was not found unworthy of the great Talbot, when he was captive to the French and they proposed to exchange him for a common man: —

'Which I disdaining scorned, and cravèd death
Rather than I would be so vile esteemed.'

Sense of honor takes strange forms in man, all the world over."

"You will leave the black man nothing peculiar but his virtues. My prejudices have so often stood rebuked before these, that they are not capable of a new shock from that quarter. I have learned to think him unrivalled in the love that seeketh not its own, that suffereth long and is kind. I remember to have heard, in my childhood, of the great disinterestedness of a black man whom I sometimes saw at my father's house. Since I have been travelling in a slave country, I have heard instances of the same sort which have surprised and touched me."

Here I related to Colvil a story which I had heard a short time before, of a slave who had been liberated by his master and had established himself in a Free State. He acquired property. His master lost his, and died, leaving two children unprovided for. His old servant made himself their guardian, gave them an education, and, continuing to toil at his trade, supplied them with the means of maintaining their position. He did this through a third person, their relation, on whom he enjoined secrecy as to the source of their revenue, that the young men might not suffer from a sense of obligation to so humble a person.

"But do you know," I continued, after I had finished my narration, "that there are those who see in this very disinterestedness of the negro in regard to the white man a proof of conscious inferiority? I have heard this asserted by some of your planters. It is an instinct, they say, similar to that which binds some of the inferior animals to man; self-respect, the sense of his own value, forbids the Anglo-Saxon to lose himself in another; the Roman sacrificed himself for nothing less than his country."

"I have heard this theory maintained," replied Colvil, "by an amiable and generous man. He used to assert that selfishness is our first duty in transactions with subordinates. 'We admire,' he would say, 'the dog who gives his life to his master; but what should we say of a man who devoted himself for his dog? The inferior knows his place by instinct, and feels himself exalted by having something to offer to the superior, who, on his part, takes but his due, and confers in honor more than he gains in convenience.' He brought forward, in confirmation of his opinion, the disinterestedness of women, who make their small sphere seem ample, since there is room for a large generosity to move in it. His tone grew tender in the course of this illustration, and he ended by telling me of his mother, of her trials, her fortitude, her self-forgetfulness. The good man had more of his mother in him than he knew. While he spoke, I was smiling to myself at the recollection that he had shown himself capable of gratitude to a slave. He afterwards, on a very trying occasion, gave proof of a disinterestedness which, if he had faith in his own theory, must have been humiliating to look back upon. Fortunately, it is harder for a man to pervert his nature than his judgment.

"Happily for human nature, examples of that loyalty, of that self-sacrifice of man to man, which is the type of and the preparation for absolute devotion to the All-Perfect, are found in every race and every rank. When I was reading in the 'Talisman' the scene between De Vaux and the raging Richard, I remembered to have seen a negro slave withstand an unreasonable master with the same courage and the same humility. Do you recollect?

"'Thou art a false traitor, De Vaux! I would I were strong enough to dash thy brains out with my battle-axe!'

"'I would you had the strength, my liege, and would risk its being so employed. The odds would be great in favor of Christendom, were Thomas Multon dead and Richard himself again.'

"The eminence of the negro race in the Christian virtues has almost brought them into discredit in our time, but it has no monopoly of them. Shakspeare had known a servant as entire in his self-devotion as your liberated slave: —

'I have five hundred crowns,
The thrifty hire I saved under your father.
Take that, and He that doth the ravens feed,
Yea, providently caters for the sparrow,
Be comfort to my age! Here is the gold.

All this I give you. Let me be your servant.
Though I look old, yet I am strong and lusty.
I'll do the service of a younger man,
In all your business and necessities.'

"I have lately been looking over the accounts of persons who have received the Montyon prize for fidelity to masters or superiors. M. Magi, of Marseilles, had in his service, when he lost his fortune in one of the French revolutions, a servant, not only as disinterested, but as poor in spirit as the most grateful negro slave. This man supported his aged master until his own infirmities rendered him almost incapable of work. He then applied to a *bureau de charité* for assistance, and devoted all that he received to his master, whose name he would not allow to be inscribed on the list of the poor, though he could thus have doubled the allowance.

"Among the persons to whom the Montyon prize has been adjudged for devotion to their masters is one man who gave proof not only of the gentler, but of the heroic virtues. This man was a negro, — a slave on a sugar-plantation in St. Domingo, — by name Eustache. When the Revolution broke out, he rescued his master, M. Belin de Villeneuve, and conducted him, together with a number of other planters who had likewise placed themselves under his protection, through infinite dangers, to a seaport, where they all embarked for the United States. The vessel in which they sailed was taken by a privateer. Eustache is not discouraged. He organizes a plot to retake the vessel. While the captors are carousing, he falls upon them at the head of the colonists, and makes them prisoners in their turn. He carried the vessel safely into Baltimore. News came that order was reëstablished in St. Domingo. The party returned, still under the guidance of Eustache. As they landed, they were attacked by the insurgents. Eustache again succeeded in rescuing his master and in conducting him to a place of safety. He now devoted himself wholly to the care of M. Belin, who was very old, and whose sight soon became so much impaired that he could no longer enjoy the solace of books. Eustache had never learned to read. He felt deeply his inability to soothe the sleepless nights of his infirm master. Nothing seemed to be impossible to his resolution. He obtained instruction privately, and one day appeared, newspaper in hand, ready to let in the outer world once more upon the solitude of the poor old man. In return for his devotion, his master gave him his freedom; but Eustache did not feel himself released from his service until death came between them. He then went to Paris, where he might at length have lived for himself. 'But he had acquired the habit of beneficence,' says the account I have seen, and could not live without indulging it. His master had provided for him out of the little remnant of his fortune. He devoted this money, and, when it was gone, his earnings, to the support of poor widows, of the sick, of workmen out of employment. When he was spoken to on the subject of his good deeds, and learned, through the surprise they called forth, that he had been doing something strange and beautiful, he put away from him the praise that was offered: 'It is not for men; I do it for the Master above.' The medal of honor was obtained for him, and his good deeds were recorded, to give an example to others, not as a reward to himself."

"St. Domingo must have been a land of heroes," I exclaimed,—"of Christian heroes. I have known a man, a slave, from that island, who, if there had been a foundation like that of Montyon in this country, would certainly have received the prize by acclamation,—unless, indeed, there were more of the same stamp whose virtues remain unrecorded, as his probably will. I have seen this man at our house in my childhood. He did not come there as a distinguished guest; he was a hair-dresser, my poor hero. Perhaps the interest in the negro race that you discover in me is in some degree due to him; for he is associated with recollections of my mother. I have often watched his dark fingers, as they were busy with the soft curls that shaded her sweet, pale face. I never saw him after her death, but I have learned his history from my father, and I have heard anecdotes of him from other persons. He, like your Eustache, left St. Domingo at the time of the Revolution. He came to New York with his master and mistress, and served them there, until, by the death of his master, his mistress was left entirely dependent upon him. He learned to dress hair in order to support her, and had such success that he was able to supply her, not only with comforts, but with many of the expensive luxuries to which she had been accustomed. When it was suggested to him that he would do well to buy his freedom, he would not hear of it; his mistress, he said, could now feel that she had a right to his services, but, if he were a free man, they might impose on her a sense of obligation. Another anecdote that I have heard of him shows that he had all the delicacy as well as the generosity of your Marseilles servant. A friend of his former master arrived in New York, after many wanderings, with little to rely upon but his Creole insouciance and self-complacency. Our hair-dresser heard his name by chance, and recognized it as that of a guest at his master's table. He sought him out, found that he was living in a pretty good apartment, but on a very spare diet. He knew the tastes of the stranger, and, without introducing himself into his presence, returned at once to his own house, and engaged his wife to employ her skill in the preparation of a dinner for his old master's friend. The dinner was sent; and this attention was repeated on several successive days, with all precautions for concealing the name of the sender. When the system was fairly under way, he went to pay his respects to the new-comer, as if he had just heard of his arrival, and inquired respectfully how he found himself in New York. The stranger told him that he was getting on very well. 'My arrival here has become known,' he said, 'and the authorities let me want for nothing.' Our friend went home to exult with his wife over the success of his stratagem. It was through her that the story became known. She used to tell it confidentially, with much enjoyment of its humor, — but not, indeed, until many years after the victim of this pious fraud had left New York."

"'Blessed are the poor in spirit!'"

"It appears that it is the easier to practise the charity that seeketh not her own, the less we have of our own to look after," I suggested.

"Yes, — it would seem that this large-heartedness

has been especially bestowed upon those whose earthly ambitions and hopes have a limit which cannot be passed over. It is the answer to that question of the seemingly disinherited children of the Great Parent: 'Hast thou but one blessing, my Father?'"

"Yet this man," I went on, after answering some questions which Edward put to me in regard to my St. Domingo hero, "yet this man appeared to be of pure African descent. His features were of the negro cast, though he had an agreeable countenance. Have not these people made an extraordinary advance in their servitude? Cannot the attainment of such a height of virtue, at only the remove of a generation or two from the most frightful barbarism, almost reconcile us to slavery?"

"If the result you suppose were proved, it might, indeed, do something towards consoling us."

"Is not this bondage, in fact, a guardianship exercised by an elder, stronger race over a weaker one for the benefit of both?"

"If we could only be sure that the restraining hand of the guardian would be withdrawn as soon as his ward attained majority!

"The man of whom you speak had undoubtedly been brought up under good influences. Others of his race, who have been placed in like favorable circumstances, have made great progress even in slavery. They have been made acquainted with a pure and elevating religion. But for this to be a benefit to them, they must already have been in a condition to receive it. If it had sought them, under its own benign aspect, in their first home, it would have found the same welcome. It is far more congenial to the negro African than the Mahometan creed which is now violently supplanting Paganism.

" The portion of Africa occupied by black peoples is of vast extent, and contains numerous nations and tribes, exhibiting marked diversities of character, and standing at different grades of civilization. The ideas current among us in regard to the negroes of Africa have been drawn chiefly from accounts we have heard of peoples living near the most frequented coasts, who have been subjected to corrupting influences from without, to which their degradation is to be attributed, rather than to inherent depravity or stupidity. The traveller finds, as he advances into the country, the people of finer personal appearance, of gentler manners; they are more hospitable, more industrious, more honest. When Central Africa has been fully laid open to the world, as there is now a prospect that before many years it will be, we shall be called upon to revise many of our opinions. I am convinced that the result of the exploring expeditions which England is now constantly sending out, and which English persistence will not suffer to slacken until their end is attained, will be an increased respect for the African.

"Among the travellers who have already published their accounts of Africa, we find that the most trustworthy and those who have had the best means of information are those who make the most favorable report. Men of cultivation and refined habits, who have penetrated far enough to see the real African, feel no contempt for his society. Park says he spent a very pleasant forenoon with the headman of the village of Samee, — who had invited a party of his friends to dine with the white man, — and that he readily accepted his invitation to stay until the cool of the evening; the company of the village Dooty and his guests being 'the more acceptable, as their gentle manners offered a striking contrast to the rudeness and barbarity of the Moors.' Clapperton, leaving Sackatoo, says of his parting with the minister of the Felatah chief, — 'I went to take leave of my old friend, the Gadado, for whom I felt the same regard as if he had been one of my oldest friends in England.' When, after a short absence, Laing returned to Falaba, — where he had passed some weeks, — he found that this capital had all the 'charms of home.' 'I felt,' he says, 'that sort of contented happiness which men feel when returning to the comforts of their own home.' He adds, that 'he is proud to acknowledge that he spent with this people, [the Sulimas,] and their neighbors, many happy days, without casting one longing thought towards more refined society or the enjoyments of England.' He speaks in the highest terms of the enlightenment and good sense of their king, — 'as honest-hearted a man,' he says, 'as ever existed,' — of his impartial justice, of the dignified simplicity of his manners. When he parted from this good old man, he says, — 'I felt as if I had parted from a father.' Read what Denham says of the inhabitants of the interior, — of their industry, their skill in weaving and dyeing, of their love of music and poetry. Above all, hear his testimony to the gentleness and simplicity of their manners."

Here Edward rose and took a volume from the bookcase.

"This is what he says, when taking his last leave of Negroland: — 'If it should be thought I have spoken too favorably of the natives, I can only answer that I have described them as I found them, — hospitable, kind-hearted, honest, and liberal. To the latest hour of my life I shall remember them with affectionate regard; and many are the untutored children of Nature in Central Africa who possess feelings and principles that would do honor to the most civilized Christian.' "

" I can understand this feeling," I said. " I have frequently felt myself moved to gratitude by the genuine kindness of these poor people, since I have been travelling about here alone; but I attributed it to their Christian training, not to their African heart."

" Some of the most disinterested, as well as some of the most intelligent black men I have known," replied Colvil, " have been native Africans. When I first came into this Southern country, where there was so much that was new to me in scenery, in natural productions, in manners, all had a charm, even the most common things showing themselves to me under a new form. But nothing attracted me so much as this strange race, with which I then first came into communication. I took great pleasure in drawing out the old legends which had been handed down to them by their foreign ancestors, and in tracing the African tradition in their customs and superstitions. When I have had the good-fortune to meet with a native African, I have tried to extract from him the history of his life, and such particulars as he might retain in his memory of the customs of his native place. It has often been a slow process. For I have remarked, that, of all slaves, the native African is the most distrustful and the least communicative. The higher sort shroud themselves in a proud silence; the lower hide under a mask of dull indifference. I do not know whether this is the case with them when they first fall into servitude, or whether it is a lesson learned from experience; for most of the native slaves I have met had already known bondage in South America or in the West Indies. Their confidence, however, once granted, is given fully and freely. I have remarked that they bestow their affection reluctantly on one of the tyrant race, but that, when it is gained, their fidelity is inflexible.

"Some of the most inert and sullen-looking negroes in the work-field have been among my best instructors. Their whole aspect has been changed for me as soon as they came to a perception of real sympathy. I have found sensibility and manliness where I had seen only stolidity and stupid endurance. From some of these men I have gathered particulars in regard to the customs and principles which prevailed in the place of their birth quite inconsistent with the character of an imbruted or even an entirely savage people.

"I have met with men of the superior tribes who have given me information in regard to the constitution of some of the negro states which filled me with surprise, so much did these accounts differ from the ideas commonly entertained of African incapacity for civil and political organization. Civilization would seem among these peoples to follow very much the same path as on other continents. Republics are found there maintaining themselves side by side with monarchy in various stages. There are federal republics, each state having its own elective chief, and all owing allegiance to one common elective head. The people there are not ignorant of the words 'rights' and 'privilege'; they withstand encroachment; they are on their guard against innovation. My conversations with these men have often recalled to me a passage in De Gerando's instructions to the traveller in countries inhabited by savage nations: —

"'The explorer of these remote regions,' he says, 'journeys in the past. With each step he passes over a century. These peoples, whom our ignorant vanity despises, are, in fact, monuments of antiquity more worthy to interest us than those of brick or stone, which tell of the idle ambition or transient power of an individual; for they retrace for us the condition of our own ancestors and the first history of the world.'

"The knowledge I gained from these natives of Africa enabled me to understand better the accounts given by travellers in that country, and to appreciate their views. The remarkable coincidences between the customs of Africa and those of ancient Europe have not been overlooked. Laing draws a parallel between the customs of Sulimana and those of ancient Rome. Bowdich has remarked the similarity of some of the religious observances of the Africans to those of Greece and Italy.

" I have, indeed, been much impressed with the resemblance that what we call their superstitions bear to those of the imaginative peoples whose childhood has furnished the world with legends that have not yet ceased to charm.

> 'The fair humanities of old religion,
> The power, the beauty, and the majesty,
> That had their haunts in dale, or piny mountain,
> Or forest, by slow stream, or pebbly spring,'

still live in the faith of Africa. 'Almost every place,' Denham says, 'has its charm or wonder.' The Africans have their genii, good and bad, their sacred groves and fountains; they have their soothsayers and sibyls, their invulnerable heroes.

"Here is a genuine African story of recent date.

" The Sheikh of Bornou made war against a neighboring state. One of the great champions of the assailed nation was Dummatoon, who put to flight whole squadrons with his single arm. He had fought hand to hand with the Sheikh himself, who had hardly escaped with life. But Dummatoon's fate found him. He was taken prisoner and brought unarmed into the presence of his great enemy. — 'You are a humbler man now, Dummatoon, than a year ago.' — 'Does my look say so? It speaks false. You should see my heart.' — 'You have done me much harm,' the Sheikh said, 'but promise me your service and I give you life.' — 'Give me death; I have deserved it of you. Give it with your own hand, if you dare to strike.' — The Sheikh made a sign to his attendants. They dragged out the prisoner, but soon returned. Neither sword nor spear would pierce him; even fire-arms failed. The Sheikh consulted his books. 'He is charmed against iron, fire, and water. Wood will kill him.' — The slaves advanced upon Dummatoon with their clubs. 'I see my death coming,' he said, and offered no more resistance.

"If the scene of this story had been laid in the heroic or the chivalric age of our world, would it have been found out of place?"

"The most obsolete part of it might be brought nearer to us: witness the 'frozen' men of Germany."

"Yes, — the Austrian rebel, Willinger, might furnish a parallel to Dummatoon. It is related of him, that 'the stroke of a cannon-ball made him recoil seven paces without killing him.'"

"Wallenstein was believed bullet-proof by his soldiers; so was Tilly."

"The army of Gustavus Adolphus was not more advanced, if we may judge by the laws of their leader. One of the chief articles in his code, according to Harte, prohibited the 'enchanting of the human body so as to render it invulnerable.' Offenders were to be strictly punished 'according to the laws of the land and those of Scripture.'"

"Yet those times thought themselves enlightened!"

"Yes, — Schiller makes Max Piccolomini even then regret the passing away of the 'old fable-beings.' From Africa 'the charming race' has not yet 'wandered out.'"

"But the superstitions of Africa are not all of the fascinating or of the heroic stamp."

"No more than those of Europe. Even in the most barbarous customs of the most barbarous tribes we are forced to recognize the African relationship to the nations from which we derive our civilization, and even to our own ancestors. When we are revolted by some tale of sanguinary superstition, we forget that the darkest rites of the most benighted worship have belonged to the early religion of the most favored countries of Europe and

Asia. At least, these things take quite another aspect for us, when viewed as the subject of antiquarian lore or of primeval poetry. If one of our missionaries should come upon an African Jephthah or Idomeneus engaged in the performance of his vow, would the position of the father be deemed tragic or monstrous? Suppose the account of the osier giants and their contents were found in the commentaries of a modern traveller in Africa, instead of in those of the explorer of Gaul, with what a different horror should we read it! Transfer the great festival of Upsala to Ashanti and call it the Yam Custom, how the poetical fades and the revolting deepens! Would not our imagination find the selfish old king Aun quite at home in Dahomey, obtaining, by the sacrifice of his nine sons, the privilege of adding the years taken from their lives to his own? Might not the legend of 'The Two Dusky Birds of Gwenddolen' have been as well a Beninish as a British tradition?

"When the Africans begin to collect their floating poetry and our literature is enriched with a translation of some Fantee epic, we shall read, perhaps, of a chief consoling the shade of his dead companion in arms by the solemn sacrifice of twelve Portuguese, French, or English prisoners reserved for the purpose. Will the tenderness of feeling and the beauty of imagery with which the inspired bard may have described the grief of the bereavement and the pomp of the funeral celebration leave us fascinated with the chief actor in the scene? The name of Achilles is still with us the synonyme of hero!"

"Indeed," I could not but admit, "I believe our opinion of African refinement would not be raised, if we found that human sacrifices were not only a rite of their religion, but a favorite subject with their poets. I remember my old school-friend Virgil does not fear to shock his countrymen by making the pious Æneas reserve eight captives to be sacrificed on the funeral pile of Pallas."

"His countrymen had no occasion to go back to their founder for examples of these sacrifices. Their Forum Boarium was there to witness to the baffling of a prophecy by a terrible mockery. Human sacrifices form the frequent subject of Greek and Italian bas-reliefs. These were, indeed, illustrations of poems and dramas. Five of the tragedies of Euripides are founded on this custom. Nor is it strange that his imagination should have been so much impressed by it; for the place and day of his birth were marked by a solemnity of this kind. He must, in his childhood, have often heard, among the other details of the Battle of Salamis, the story of the royal captives, with their stately beauty and their splendid dress, brought in at the moment of the preparatory sacrifices, when instantly the flame, darting up bright and clear, demanded them, and a sneeze on the right confirmed their fate! Greece witnessed this spectacle, not Africa.

"The modern stage does not entirely exclude from the elements of the tragic this fearful recognition of the principle of expiation. Even the musical drama ventures with an antique subject to revive the ancient horror. In a play which I have here, by a new English dramatist, the idea of this cruel atonement reappears, though in a softened form. The hero offers up his life upon the altar to avert a curse from his country. Ought we to be very much surprised, since the tradition of what was once a universal fact has not yet wholly died out with us, if there are spots in Africa where the custom itself has lingered, as it continued to exist in Gaul, Britain, and still later in Scandinavia, after the more civilized countries of Europe had rejected it?"

"Eyes have we, yet we see not!"

"The religious ceremonies of the Africans," Edward continued, "bear, even in detail, an extraordinary resemblance to those of Greece and Italy. For example, as the Romans sacrificed white victims to the celestial, and black to the infernal gods, so some nations of Africa offer white animals on joyful, black on mournful occasions. The veneration in which the serpent is held by the negroes of Africa, and its significance as the emblem of healing, are other coincidences. Some customs of modern Europe which have come down from a remote period are in full force in Africa, — such as pilgrimages to sacred shrines in order to merit or give thanks for divine favors, religious processions to obtain rain, and so forth. A Moravian missionary reports that certain African peoples offer, as we do, grace before meat: 'O God, thou hast made this to grow!' More grateful than we, they give thanks also before work: 'O God, thou hast given me this strength!' The prayer of the Watje woman does not differ much from Pope's Universal Prayer, except in being more concise: 'O God, I know thee not, but thou knowest me; give me what I need!'

"Certainly some of the customs of the Africans are puerile enough in our eyes: such as their being governed in an important decision by the flight of a bird to the right or left; their pouring out on the ground a little liquor before they drink, as an offering to some invisible divinity; their listening for oracles from a cave or a prophetic tree. Yet for all these follies we know there are respectable precedents. So there are for the custom of offering food to tutelary beings and to the spirits of the dead, which seems to us so childish and to show such gross ideas of the other world. I know no custom which has more excited the pity and scorn of travellers than this. Yet here the negro belief is kept in countenance, not only by the youthful time of the most honored races, but by one of the first minds of an enlightened age, — by the greatest poet who has devoted his genius to the illustration of our own religious faith. Adam invites Raphael timidly to the banquet that Eve has set out for them; he fears it may be

> 'Unsavory food, perhaps,
> To spiritual natures.'

Raphael reassures him: —

> 'What He gives —
> Whose praise be ever sung — to man, in part
> Spiritual, may of purest spirits be found
> No ingrateful food: and food alike those pure
> Intelligential substances require,
> As doth your rational; and both contain
> Within them every lower faculty
> Of sense, whereby they hear, see, smell, touch, taste.
> . . . . . . So down they sat,
> And to their viands fell, not seemingly
> The angel nor in mist, — the common gloss
> Of theologians, — but with keen despatch
> Of real hunger.'

Shall we feel contempt for the African because he attributes to the spirits of his friends a complaisance which the sublimest of epic poets finds not unworthy of an archangel? No, let us not despise these simple peoples too much. Their observances often symbolize and preserve great truths, and we are often made to feel that the inspiration of cultivated genius hardly informs more definitely than their humble intuition."

The solid German had, already for the second time since our conversation began, passed by the window with a slow step. I did not feel called upon to interpret this manœuvre, and Edward probably thought, as I did, that my rival would soon enough have everything his own way again; for, after a glance of hesitation, he turned back to me. He gave me, in answer to my questions, many particulars in regard to the religious observances of different tribes of Africans. I received from him afterwards, in the course of our correspondence, fuller information; but this belongs to another period of our acquaintance. I noted in my journal, at that time, only the facts and illustrations that especially struck my fancy. I remember his telling me, however, that, although the Pagan Africans believed in a great number of divinities of different grades, yet the idea of one God supreme over all had been found to exist even among the most barbarous tribes.

"I know," he said, "there are hasty travellers who deny this. I have met with one who asserted of a certain tribe through whose territory he had passed, that 'they had no religion at all, and no idea of the existence of a God.' — 'Do they never offer any kind of worship?' some one present asked. — 'Oh, they pray when they are in distress, but they don't know what they pray to.' — This is an example of the rashness of superficial travellers.

" The fact is, that the African is reserved in conversation with strangers on religious topics; his awe of the unseen is great, and he does not dare to treat these subjects with familiarity. Park found among the negro people with which he was best acquainted a belief, not only in a God, but in a future state of rewards and punishments, universal. But he says it is difficult to make them converse on these subjects, and that, in particular, when questioned in regard to their ideas of a future life, 'they express themselves with reverence, but endeavor to shorten the discussion.' I have heard the same thing from persons who have been in Africa, and their statements have been confirmed by my own experience of the reserve of the native African on these subjects."

From the religion of the Africans I drew Colvil to their manners and characteristics.

" I have perhaps been misled by such superficial travellers as you speak of, or by my own superficial reading of better ones; but I have received an impression, that, among the African tribes, the bond of nationality, and even the ties of blood, are weaker than they commonly are in the early time of the superior races."

"I believe," Colvil answered, "the testimony of the most judicious travellers will not be found to confirm this impression. Park says, emphatically, that, whatever difference there may be between the European and African in features and skin, 'there is none in the genuine sympathies and characteristics of our common nature.' How pleasing is the account he gives of the reception of his blacksmith guide, on his return home after an absence of four years! His brother comes out to meet him, bringing a horse, that he may enter his native place with the more dignity, and accompanied by a minstrel, who leads the way into the town, singing the praises and welcome of the restored citizen. The townspeople flock round him, exulting and congratulating; but when they approach his home, all make way for the old blind mother, who, unable to see her son, passes her trembling hands over his face and listens intently for his voice. The white man is overlooked; it is not until the regained son and brother, seated in the midst of his family, has given his history in full from the day of his departure, and, arriving at the place where the stranger has a part in it, points him out to them, that the attention of the household is directed to him. Then he appears to them like 'a being dropped from the clouds,' so unconscious have they been of his presence. Read the account given by Captain Tuckey, and again by Professor Smith, of the joy of the Congo father, on recovering his lost son, stolen from him, under disguise of friendship, eleven years before, — a joy, the ardor of which proved, so says the Professor, 'that, even among this people, Nature is awake to tender emotions.' Such remarks as this call up a sad smile, like the bull of Paul Third, which decreed souls to the American Indians."

"But is it not true that there are tribes in Africa who sell their own countrymen, and even their relatives, into slavery?"

"Is this without a parallel among the Caucasian peoples? Not to go back to Joseph's brethren, nor to the Thracians, who, Herodotus tells us, sold their own children, let us look in Christian times at nearer nations. Charlemagne called the attention of Pope Adrian to the sale of Italians by their own countrymen to foreigners, and the Pope could only answer, that he had done everything in his power to prevent this traffic, but without success, since it took place under the pressure of famine. Britain, like Africa, once supplied foreign slave-markets; she has herself dealt in her own sons;

and the reproach has been brought against Christian England as freely as against heathen Africa, that the young brother was not safe from the avarice of the elder, nor the tender child from the parent's. I fear this baseness was not entirely unknown even among the free, manly peoples of Scandinavia, from whom we are proud to derive our origin. Not half a century ago, a ballad which records an act of this sort was still sung on the shores of Lake Wetter: —

'My father and my mother, oh, they have suffered need!
They sold me away for a little bit of bread,
All into the heathenish country, there to perish!'

"In times of famine, men in Africa have been known to sell themselves, in order, with the price of their freedom, to provide for those dependent on them; parents have at such times, perhaps, even sold their own children into bondage. But it is to be remembered that the species of serfdom which exists in Africa, among the negro nations, bears no resemblance to slavery as we know it. The African bondman has rights; he is a member of the community, protected by the laws. He is completely disfranchised only when he passes from his Pagan master to his Christian owner. In negro Africa the master cannot sell his bondman, except for crime of which he shall have been duly convicted by public trial. Such is the law of African slavery, according to Mungo Park. Laing makes the same statement. Even in Congo — which seems to have been almost more than any other part of Africa depraved and ruined by the slave-trade — Tuckey found that the domestic slave was not subject to sale. Captives taken in war, and men who have incurred slavery as a penalty, are excepted from these privileges; but only in their own persons; their children have the rights of domestic bondmen. The African serf has generally light work and gentle treatment. Park says, that, in all labors, mechanic or agricultural, the master is seen working with the bondman, 'without any distinction of superiority.' As Murray sums it up: 'The slavery of African to African is comparatively mild. The labor required in this state of society is not such as to impose suffering or exhaustion; the slave sits on the same mat with his master, eats out of the same dish, and talks with him as with an equal.' It is the foreign trade in men that has introduced those elements of horror which make us shudder at the words, African Slavery. The continual wars which desolate the country, and which have destroyed or carried back into barbarism many flourishing nations that had made great advances in the arts of cultivated life, are almost always undertaken to supply this demand from without. The terror with which the knowledge of their destination fills the poor captives taken in war or kidnapped, leading them to make constant attempts at escape, has occasioned a fearful severity on the part of the slave-dealers. The poor victims are often forced to march heavily ironed. The horrors of the inland passage are sometimes almost equal to those of the slave-ship."

"And who is responsible for this?" I could not help exclaiming; "this foreign trade is not an African invention."

"No; the cupidity of the white races introduced and sustains it. This trade has dried up the sources of honorable commerce; wherever it has established itself, it has stifled the native virtues of the African and stimulated his baser propensities, — developing, where its influences are concentrated, a frightful depravity."

"And we hear the report of this, and judge the negro worthy of no better fate than he finds!"

"The Christian tempter decrees the Pagan man-seller the portion which the weak tool receives from the powerful villain who takes the profit of a misdeed and leaves to his accomplice the opprobrium and the penalty.

"It is remarkable that those unfortunate countries whose debasement and sanguinary superstitions have made the name of Africa a byword lie within the limits of the Guinea of old time, whose mythical fame lured Henry of Portugal, and where his countrymen first planted the traffic which was to become Africa's curse — and ours. Congo, Calabar, are equally notorious as the marts of this trade and as the scenes of revolting rites; Ashanti is near the coast which first realized the golden dreams of the Portuguese; Dahomey lies within that which bears the ill-omened name of the Slave-Coast. In these countries a barbarous despotism has taken the place of the milder governments of the interior and less corrupted regions. Parts of the eastern coast and the country lying along the Zambesi have suffered deeply from the same causes. But even in the most fallen of these doomed countries the near observer finds the remains of the virtues of a better time, and the magnanimity which marks the negro character often shines out among the gloomy traits."

"Are the negroes themselves sensible of the evils this trade brings upon them?"

"The travellers who have taken the most pains to ascertain the feeling of Africa on this subject affirm that it is disapproved by the people at large, — though it may be regarded with indifference by those who are thoroughly debased by it. Its suppression is opposed by the kings and chiefs who derive a revenue from it, and by a few rich men who have fattened on it. The more enlightened of the rulers, however, are already sensible of the evils it entails on their people, and are desirous to see an honest and humane trade take its place. Tuckey reported in 1816 that even in Congo the people at large 'assuredly desire the abolition of this trade.' He says that every man he conversed with told him, that, if the white men did not come for slaves, the practice of kidnapping would cease. Denham expresses his belief that this traffic is seen with 'a disgust which habit cannot conquer,' by the people of Bornu, whither great numbers of slaves are brought to be delivered up to the foreign traders, who will take nothing else in exchange for their wares. The country he explored was disturbed by continual incursions made by Mahometan tribes on their Pagan neighbors. They abstained from enslaving those who had been converted to their own faith: 'Believers,' they say, 'do not bind each other.' The conquering state often imposes a yearly tribute of slaves on the subjected one, which, to spare its own people, again makes inroads upon a neighbor; thus the miseries of the slave-trade are carried far inward, to nations which have had no part in its crimes.

"I knew, a few years ago, an African from the interior, who had been carried off in a foray of this sort, made by a people who were not at enmity with his own. His love for his country was intense. He described it to me as a perfect Paradise. The accounts he gave me of the modes of tillage in use there, of the fields waving with grain, the groves of fruit-trees, the comfortable houses, the gentle manners of the people, proved a state of things far removed from barbarism. He died in the belief, that, as soon as his soul left its captive body, it would be born again in his own land."

"Had he not been converted?"

"He was a fervent believer in the life and death of Christ and in his doctrines. But I do not know whether he could have been accepted as an orthodox convert; for, as is usual with native Africans, he retained many of his early religious ideas, which, indeed, he used to defend very skilfully by arguments drawn from Scripture. He believed in tutelary spirits, and in the power of evil demons to tempt and injure. He contended that this faith was quite consistent with the Christian teaching, as also his belief that the soul could return to earth. He thought the permission to see his home again had been accorded to him as a special grace, in compensation for his misfortunes; for, he said, he could not enjoy heaven until this great longing of his soul had been satisfied. He affirmed that his people were already in possession of some of the great truths of Christianity; that they practised the laws of love and forgiveness; but they did not know who had brought these to earth, nor whom they ought to thank for them. He was to give them a knowledge of their Benefactor. This man's health had been broken by his sufferings in the slave-ship and by severe usage after he left it. Fortunately, he passed into the hands of a kind master before he had suffered the worst injuries that slavery inflicts. He had been in the power of those who could kill the body, but they had not destroyed his soul. He retained his affectionate nature, and was simple and truthful. But he was very imaginative, and his accounts of distant scenes and occurrences may have been colored and enriched without his being conscious of it."

"It is unfortunate," I said, "that, in colonies established in Africa for the benefit of the black race, men whose characters have been enfeebled, if not perverted, by servitude, must, at least in the beginning, make so large an element. I once knew a man, a very good man in his way, who had formed a theory in regard to the incapacity and irredeemable worthlessness of negroes from experiences he had had in some settlement, I forget now what one, near the coast. He said of the blacks composing it, that they were all thieves and liars, — destitute, in fact, of all moral principle; and this, 'although they had all been slaves, and had thus enjoyed the advantages of discipline and training.'"

"And no doubt this man passed for an authority, as one who had seen the blacks in their own country."

"Yes,—his opinions were considered conclusive in a large circle. When I questioned him a little,—for I was not one of the best-convinced,—he admitted that these same people were kind and hospitable, and that they 'were honest enough among themselves.'"

"The principle of having one code for themselves and another for their dealings with aliens has not only been learned by the Africans in their enslavement, it was very early taught them by the foreign traders. Purchas gives, in his 'Pilgrims,' an account of the Gold and Grain Coasts in 1601, written by a Dutch trader. He says of the natives,—'At first, they were very simple in their dealings, and trusted the Netherlanders very much; at which we wondered. For they thought that white men were gods and would not deceive them.' So, he relates very coolly, 'we used to deceive them, selling them rotten cloth and short measure, patched basins, and knives so rusty that they could not be drawn without breaking, and such like wares.' The golden harvest did not last long, however. 'For now,' he presently says, 'they have such skill in our wares that they almost go beyond us.' The poor natives learned yet other lessons. By the time our Netherlander left their country, he had no better opinion of them than your friend had of the colony of liberated slaves. 'For stealing,' he says, 'of all the nations in the world, they have not their masters.' He finds them 'full of untruth,' and so shameless that they are only proud of deceiving and cheating him and his comrades. 'For,' he says, 'they think us crafty men, and that they show themselves the craftier when they take us in.' But he, too, adds, — 'They think it shame to steal from each other, and what promises they make among themselves they keep well.' Honest Purchas furnishes the African voyages with marginal notes such as these: — 'White devils can hardly make black saints': Let not heathens be made worse by Christians, which, alas! is now common in all remote parts.'"

"I am afraid these notes are hardly yet obsolete."

"Two hundred years after the Netherlander's voyage, this system of bad faith on the part of Europeans was found in full force in its darkest form, — and yet the natives not wholly cured of their confidence in the white men! Bowdich tells us, that, when African chiefs, desirous of giving their sons a Christian education, have intrusted them to English captains who promised to take them to England for this purpose, these children 'have invariably been sold as slaves'! The young man I spoke of just now, whom Tuckey restored to his father, 'a prince of the blood,' in Congo, had been thus confided to a Liverpool captain, who engaged to take him to England and have him instructed, but who sold him as a slave at St. Kitt's."

"And I have heard the distrust of the negroes of Africa, and their slowness to believe that the Christian missionaries had come among them solely to benefit them, attributed to their own brutal selfishness, which incapacitated them even for conceiving of disinterested kindness!"

"The humanity and gentleness of the negroes are proved — if by nothing else — by the security with which the white man can still travel among them and live with them, after all the evils he has brought upon their country, and the daily instances of perfidy and depravity he is exhibiting there. That they do not give their confidence to any individual of this race, until after a long experience, shows only that they are not so wanting in judgment and discretion as has been pretended.

"Some of the coarser misrepresentations," Colvil continued, "and tales of African horror, spread by rash or wonder-loving voyagers, have been fully discredited by more sober and judicious explorers: as, for example, the stories of cannibalism, which would appear to rest on the same authority as the accounts of tribes of men with four eyes, or with tails, or horns. Tuckey and his associates, who passed through regions rife with rumors of cannibalism, saw appearances which, if pains had not been taken to obtain an explanation, would have confirmed these reports, wholly without foundation, as it afterwards appeared. In the General Observations appended to his Narrative, which sum up the experiences and results of the expedition, the conviction is expressed that the 'many idle stories reported by the Capuchin and other missionaries to Congo, of the Giagas and Anzicas, their neighbors, delighting in human flesh, had no other foundation than their fears worked upon by the stories of the neighboring tribes.'"

"This reminds me that I once heard a shrewd sea-captain say, that missionaries were somewhat prone to believe in the existence of these atrocities among the unconverted. Perhaps they feel that it gives more importance to their work."

"If so, I think it is a mistaken view. One of the strongest reasons for carrying the blessings of our religion into Africa is that it will come to a people ready and waiting to receive it."

"I should think that there was little temptation to cannibalism in a country like Africa, where food is obtained, they say, with so little trouble."

"The people, too, use very little animal food. The uncorrupted African is sober in his diet.

"But do you know, that, in some parts of Africa, the blacks believe the whites to be a man-eating race? And really with more reason than we have for thinking them so; for they cannot otherwise account for the immense consumption of human merchandise. The terror of the poor kidnapped creatures is carried to extremity by the thought that they are to go across the water to be cooked and eaten. 'It is these white Christians with blue eyes, like the hyena's, that eat the blacks, when they have them out of their own country.' This pleasant account of himself and his like an English traveller heard given by an old woman in the interior of Africa. Clapperton found that even at Mourzuk reports of cannibalism were circulated in regard to him and his party. 'But,' he says, 'when we were better known, the prejudice wore off.'"

"When the Africans are better known, perhaps our prejudices may wear off, too."

"Clapperton had the good sense to infer that similar stories told of the people of Yacoba might be 'only idle Arab tales.' Robertson, who lived many years in Africa, declares that the stories of cannibalism are 'ridiculous.' He says, speaking of reports of this sort in regard to the people of Sonio,

—'A more preposterous or foolish opinion could not be conceived.' A trader at Bonny once told him so plausible a story about the Quas eating those that fell into their power, that he was inclined to believe it; but he was afterwards convinced that there was no truth in it. The natives often give strangers a fearful account of the dangers of the interior in order to deter them from penetrating into the country. Robertson thinks the Portuguese have propagated these tales of horror in regard to regions from which they drew profit, to prevent other foreigners from interfering with them. 'But,' he says, 'from their not having been devoured themselves, it would seem other food is plentiful.' "

"The pleasure of telling wonderful stories, with so little chance of contradiction, has probably been motive enough for many a Sindbad."

"One Andrew Battell, who was quite an authority in his time, seems to have indulged largely in this amusement. His marvellous relations, tran scribed by one book-maker after another, still find their way into compilations upon Africa.

"But, even where there is candor and good judgment, we must take for granted the probability of much misconception on the part of the foreign observer. The best travellers in Africa are English and French. Now, when we see what droll mistakes Frenchmen fall into, when writing on English manners, and that the English show an equal incapacity for understanding and describing theirs, how can we help asking ourselves whether men of either of these nations are likely to judge correctly peoples of a widely different family, with whom they can hold only the most limited and barren communication by signs, or by interpreters who have often an imperfect knowledge of both the languages they try to translate?

"See what prejudice could do, even in merry England, with a warm-hearted, quick-witted man, who was hardly a foreigner there, — for the language of the country was his own. Curran, in a letter to a friend, giving an account of a journey to Windsor, declares his belief that the 'English peasant is very little better than a Hottentot.' 'In every stupid face you meet,' he says, 'you may read more than you ever conceived of an English boor, haughty, ignorant, unsociable, credulous, unaccommodating.' Would it be possible to describe a more disagreeable savage?"

"What errors English travellers in this country fall into, though they speak our language, and their customs are similar to ours! How few, even of those who are above the imputation of unfairness, are accurate in their statements, to say nothing of their inferences!"

"Fewer still know how to approve and blame in

the right place. Englishmen, in general, respect us when we entertain the same follies they do; but are as severe on us for holding to those they have dropped as for shaking off those they still cling to. But all men are prone to judge the manners of other countries by the standard of their own, and the civilized world views from its own stand-point that which it calls savage. We find the Africans barbarians, wherever their customs differ from ours; but they are on the road to civilization, when their nonsense suits our nonsense. It is quite in order, for example, that they should bring the exhilaration of music to beguile the fatigue of a warlike march, and to strengthen the arm for devastation and murder; but when we find that the African invigorates in the same manner the nerves and muscles of the peaceful husbandman, we pity the poor, ignorant creature. Sow and reap to music! what a lazy way of going on!"

"Yet that little remnant of a golden age in Europe, the vintage-feast, we find poetical."

"Upon authority. And then the peasants of Europe are not negroes."

"I should not be sorry, if music with us made as necessary a part of daily life as it seems to be in Africa."

"When it does, we shall admire ourselves very much for it, no doubt. In the mean time, our restricted enjoyment of it is a part of our superiority.

"An English Chief-Justice of the fifteenth century states, with evident gratification to his national pride, that there are more men hung in England for crimes of violence in three years than in France in seven. He finds here a proof of the superior courage of his countrymen: — 'There are few Frenchmen hung for robbery; for they have no hearts for so terrible a deed.' 'In England,' he says, 'it has often been seen that three or four thieves have set upon seven or eight true men and have robbed them all; whereas in France seven or eight thieves are not bold enough to rob three or four true men.' A Frenchman of the time, accepting the fact, would possibly have accounted for it by the valor of the honest men of France, rather than by the cowardice of her thieves. If the Africans could hear the view taken by foreigners of some of their customs or of some points in their character, they would perhaps bring forward a plausible defence."

"Take their indolence, for example," I suggested.

"Might they not say, — It is our moderation, our humanity, that keep us from wearing out our lives, or driving others through theirs, in unceasing toil? The never-satisfied avidity of the whites, through which they lose sight of the end in the means, makes our reasonable, cheerful industry look to them like idleness.

"Might they not say,—as, indeed, Mungo Park has said for them,—that a people cannot be called indolent whose wants are supplied by its own exertions? They might perhaps go farther, and say that they show more respect for labor than we do; for they love it, they enjoy it, they fête it. With them, sowing-time is a time of festival; the harvest, again, is the season of 'an infinity of rejoicings.' The chief of the village comes out at the head of the workmen, attended by a band of minstrels, who make 'the air resound with their songs.'

"If the scene Laing saw at Falaba had been described by some old Greek poet, what a beautiful picture of primitive manners we should find it! The inhabitants of Falaba owe the king three days' labor in the year,—one to sow his rice, one to weed, and one to reap it. It was the spring festival that Laing saw. The king appeared attended by his band of minstrels to encourage the workmen. The performances began with a discourse by the chief orator. In less than a quarter of an hour after it was concluded, the men were arranged in order of work and with a method which Laing found truly astonishing. They were drawn up in two lines: the first, five hundred persons, scattered the seed; the second, about two thousand, covered it. 'They advanced,' he says, 'regularly, and with such rapidity that the work appeared more like magic than a human performance.' Their labors were accompanied by the music of the minstrels, 'without whose presence and cheering song,' as Laing says, 'nothing is effected in work, festivity, or war.'

"Are those African tribes that are renowned for their music as industrious as the others?"

"It is probable that the musicians themselves are not skilful in any art but their own. But I have not observed any connection between the African's love of music and his supposed indolence. The Timanis, who, from their position near the mouth of a large river, have been so depraved by the slave-trade that the habit of honest industry has almost died out among them, seem to have lost in an equal degree the love of genial recreation. Laing passed through their country on his way into the interior. He speaks often of their sorcerers, but says nothing of minstrels. They held no festivals in honor of the stranger, gave him no serenades, and an air of distrust made their limited hospitality yet more ungracious. But when he reached the country of the Kurankos, a people a degree higher in manners and in industry, he found the barbarian graces revive. In every town he enters the stranger receives a musical reception."

"What was the character of this music?"

"At first, rude enough. The traveller would have preferred a quiet night's rest to the noisy serenade they gave him at Kulufa, the first important Kuranko town he entered. At Simera, his next stopping-place, the song of welcome was chanted to a very rude instrument, a sort of violin, having but one string of twisted horse-hair; yet the performer 'contrived to produce a pleasing harmony.' Laing heard no music, however, captivating to a European ear, until he reached Kamato, the last Kuranko town of importance that he passed through: here he heard 'instruments skilfully handled, that sent forth most melodious sounds.' He arrived at a time of mourning. The people were lamenting the death of their chief. The crying and wailing continued through the night; but at daybreak music took their place. 'The deep tones of a large balafu resounded through the morning-air in a manner truly solemn.' 'I awoke early,' he says, 'and lay listening for upwards of an hour with pleasure to the music, which rang in my ears like magic.' The singers on this occasion were from Sangara, which lies yet farther east than the country of the Sulimas, which Laing entered on leaving the Kurankos. Here he found himself in a land of music. In the first Sulima town he entered, the inhabitants made a great feast in his honor, ending with a dance to 'the sweet music of the balafu.' The airs, he says, were 'soft and wild,' and awakened in him 'so strong a remembrance of early days,' that he was almost ready himself to 'join the merry throng.'"

"'Remembrance of early days'? Then the soft, wild airs of this African people must have recalled to Laing the melodies of Scotland!"

"Perhaps some of the beautiful airs which the Africans have given to our country were first heard in Sulimana or Sangara. As Laing passed on through the Sulima country, deputations from the towns came out to meet him, always attended by a band of music. Even a slave-town, which he passed through just before arriving at the Sulima capital, did not neglect this refined courtesy. The headman — himself a slave — sent out a band of music and fifty armed men to escort the 'king's stranger' into his town. The people of this town vied with each other in acts of kindness. The headman, whom Laing describes as 'a most respectable, venerable-looking old man,' received him warmly, and entertained him with great hospitality. Laing was glad to rest for a day in his town. The music that Laing heard among the Sulimas seems to have been all of an agreeable character, except the warlike music during a kind of sham-fight, and the terrific chorus to a war-song. He found the people of this musical land more skilled in agriculture than those of the other countries he had passed through. He saw here large plantations of rice; he was struck by the regularity and beauty of the alternate beds of corn and cassada, by the clean appearance of the ground, and the care taken to keep it free from weeds. In the rich pastures large flocks of sheep and herds of oxen were grazing."

"How far is this country from the coast?"

"The capital of the Sulimas is about two hundred miles east from the colony of Sierra Leone. Laing was the first white man who appeared in those regions."

"These people had, then, gained nothing from civilized instructors?"

"I should rather say they had not lost everything through civilized betrayers. They had suffered much from the effects of the slave-trade, though not in an equal degree with those in direct communication with the great slave-marts near the coast. The people of Sangara, which lies beyond Sulimana, seem to be as superior to the Sulimas in skill and industry as the Sulimas to the Kurankos, or these again to the Timanis. It is not in morals alone that the people in the neighborhood of foreign settlements in Africa are, as Robertson says of those on the Gold Coast, in 'a worse condition than before they ever saw the face of a European.'

"There are many indications that Africa has been arrested in her social development, — that the finer virtues and the higher forms of industry have been blighted in their expansion by the contact of our selfish civilization. It is a great debt that must be paid, — that will be paid, I trust."

It was Mrs. Colvil's low, clear voice that broke the silence in which we had been sitting for some minutes: —

"Do you remember that African lyre?"

"Yes," said Edward; and then, in answer to my inquiring look, continued: —

"We met in New York, many years ago, when we were on our way from our old home to this place, a man who had lived several years in Africa. He had brought back with him some specimens of native art, — among others, a musical instrument which should have been worth to its inventor the fame of Terpander. I asked the owner whether this instrument were really a native invention, and whether it was not probable that some hints had been given by Europeans. He assured me that it came from a 'very savage' tribe in the interior, who had never seen a white man; and added, with a smile of condescension for my boyish simplicity, — 'I don't think there have been many harps carried out to Africa; we don't go there to teach music.' The answer fell cold on my heart. It has often come back to me, when I have been reading accounts of Christian dealing in Africa. And here, when I have seen in this orphan race the struggling of undeveloped capacities or the gleams of undirected genius, I have heard, in the tones of that careless voice, the light rebuke, — We did not bring them here to teach them."

"One question more."

Edward's thoughtful look brightened, as if with a pleased surprise, at my curiosity about a subject which, I now saw, must have interested him long and deeply. It was not often, probably, that he found a sympathizer.

"One question more: The women of Africa, — is not their condition abject even among the superior tribes?"

"The life of the women is far more laborious than that of the men: they share in the duties of agriculture; the preparation of food is with them an elaborate process; they are reported to be very exact, tidy housekeepers, and to take as much pleasure in a clean floor and shining pans as old-fashioned Dutch housewives. Whatever may be thought of the industry of the men, the women of Africa are certainly not to be reproached with a want of it. But when the condition of women in what we call barbarous countries is under discussion, it seems to be taken for granted that all the women of the civilized world lead a life of elegant leisure. I am afraid there are women overworked and undervalued in Christian countries as well as in Pagan. Christianity has yet a great work to do in both. The claims of those who make no claim for themselves are everywhere the last to be recognized.

"In those parts of Africa that have been thoroughly debased by the slave-trade, the condition of the women is undoubtedly terribly degraded. Even farther inland, where the manners are less directly affected by it, its influence is felt on the standing and character of women. Laing says, with great justice, that 'the warlike and predatory life of the men, which has been fostered and confirmed into habit under the excitement of the trade in slaves, has had its usual effect in destroying the better feelings towards women.' But there are not wanting races in Africa among whom the family-relations are regulated by a higher justice, and even by a certain refinement of kindness. It is certain, that, in many parts of the country, women are treated with a respect never paid them, except when it is won by capacity and disinterestedness. It is not an unusual thing, among the nations of the interior, to see a woman elevated to the office of chief. In one important kingdom, the name of the mother is always borne with that of the father, as among the ancient Etruscans. There are nations among whom the title of the mother is considered stronger than that of the father, and, in case of a separation, the children remain with her. The most solemn oath of the Damaras is, 'By the tears of my mother!'

"Africa has had her share of heroines, from the magnificent Queen of Matamba, renowned in diplomacy and war, down to the Queen of Akim, a woman 'of almost infantile countenance and a voice low and soft as the tones of a flute,' but who, in the war against the Tiger-king of Ashantee, 'was seen everywhere in the heat of the battle, encouraging and exciting her troops; wherever the greatest danger was, there was the energetic Queen of Akim.' Holman compares her to Boadicea, and even to the great Queen Bess."

"I remember that Park speaks with respect and gratitude of the African women."

"His tribute to their kind-heartedness is familiar, because it is associated with a striking incident; but his testimony to their domestic worth is, I think, less known. He speaks in warm commendation of their maternal devotion. He saw with satisfaction that their solicitude was not confined to the physical well-being of their children. 'One of the first lessons that the Mandingo women teach their children is the practice of truth.' He saw a poor herdsman brought home mortally wounded by Moorish robbers, and witnessed the despair of the mother. 'Her only consolation,' he says, 'in her uttermost grief, was the reflection, that her poor boy, in the course of his blameless life, had never told a lie.' The affection of the African mother is fully returned. Park says he 'observed in all parts of Africa that the greatest affront which could be offered to a negro was to reflect on her who gave him birth.' 'Strike me, but do not curse my mother,' is heard, he says, even from slaves.

"According to my authority, Denham, here," continued Edward, laying his hand on the book from which he had read, "the women of Bornou have as much influence over their husbands as most Christian wives can pretend to. He tells us, that, the Sheikh having made some regulations displeasing to the women of Kouka, more than one hundred families left the place,—before, a favorite residence,—and went to live where these edicts were not in force. The women who remained omitted to appear in a religious procession in which they should have taken an important part, and the Sheikh had to put up with this affront.

"I once met with a man who had lived long in one of the Portuguese settlements in Africa, and had a good knowledge of many nations of the interior. He told me of one considerable tribe among whom the women were held in such esteem that nothing of importance was decided without their counsel. It was impossible to conclude any transaction with a man of this tribe, or engage him to perform any work, until he had obtained the approbation of his wife. I think it must be to this or to some related tribe that a young African belonged with whom I made acquaintance a few years ago. He was evidently of one of the higher races. He was only fourteen years old when he left his home, but his recollections of his early years were very distinct. He described to me the house of his father, and the garden, his mother's pride, which surrounded it. His father, he assured me, had but one wife. She died. The father then abandoned his possessions, and the family never returned to their former home, except to lay offerings on the mother's grave. He told me that this excessive respect for the dead was not peculiar to his father, but the custom of his people. Piety to the dead is, indeed, a characteristic of the Africans. After a battle, it is common for them to render the last offices to the bodies of their enemies as well as to those of their own people. They have an instinctive sense of the dignity of the human frame; though, perhaps, as yet they may have shown it only in act, and may not have found in words the perfect expression of this feeling that Spenser has furnished us with: —

> 'The wondrous workmanship of God's own mould,
> Whose face he made all beasts to fear, and gave
> All in his hand, even dead we honor should.'

"And yet, why do I say this?" he added, after a moment's thought. "Africa is a land of poets. There is probably no feeling common to humanity that they have not consecrated in their verse."

"I have seen but one translation of an African poem, — that given by Mungo Park."

"The song of the young improvvisatrice at Sego, which was paraphrased in English by the Duchess of Devonshire? Most of the poems given by travellers in Africa have been effusions of this sort, preserved on account of the occasion which called them forth: for the gift of song would seem to be as liberally bestowed in Africa as in Italy. I do not remember to have met with a translation of any of the traditionary poetry of the Africans. This must be the most valuable. Their bards are their historians, the preservers of their legends, and of the maxims which embody the wisdom of their ancestors. I do not know that we have a translation of any poem by a bard whom the Africans themselves regard as eminent.

"Laing gives a translation of a song which commemorates the successful resistance of the Sulimas to an attack upon their capital by the Fulahs. It is modern. Laing saw its hero, Yarradi, brother to the king of the Sulimas. Considering that the subject is warlike, it is of an elevated character. It contains no vituperative, no sanguinary expressions. It begins with a generous recognition of the valor of the enemy: —

"'The Fulahs are brave; only the Sulimas can stand against them. They came upon us over the hills like the rolling of a mighty river. They demanded tribute of the men of Falaba. Yarradi made answer with a barbed arrow. The fight began; the sun hid his face, that he might not see the number of the slain. The clouds that covered the sky lowered like the brow of our leader. The Fulahs fought like men. But what could they against Yarradi, the Sulima lion? They fled, never to return, and Falaba is at peace.'

"I think this poem bears the disadvantage of a plain prose translation as well as some of more illustrious origin. Suppose it invested with the charm of rhythm, and of that adaptation of the language to the ideas which the poet, to whom both were native, must have given it, and we have, I think, a patriotic poem that might stand with some to which civilized hearts have beat quicker.

"Bowdich has noted down some fragments of mythology contained in the popular poetry of the Africans. A favorite song chanted in Empoöngwa to the enchambee, in the moonlight evenings, relates the arts by which the Sun gained an ascendency over the Moon, created its equal by the common Father.

"I am sorry that Bowdich could not secure the poem he heard sung to the harp by the deformed, quivering-eyed bard from Imbiki, who, they said, 'was mad only when he played,' and who, in his recitative, 'now mournful, now impetuous, now exhilarated, wandered through the life of man and the animal and vegetable kingdoms.' At the close of one of his strophes, the strange bard 'burst out with the full force of his powerful voice in the notes of the "Hallelujah" of Händel.' Bowdich thinks that this rhapsody, 'abrupt, transient, allegorical,' was without connection or purpose. But I believe a Frenchman would pronounce the same judgment on the 'Allegro' of Milton sung to Händel's music, if he were kept informed, as Bowdich was, by an oral translation given at the time, line by line, and only half caught by an ear intent on following the music. Bowdich says he was 'so possessed by the music, that he could not note half that was communicated to him by the headman of the town, who translated for him.'

"It is much to be desired that some men possessed of the peculiar genius and the zealous industry of the Danish, German, and Finnish scholars, who have done so much to preserve the early poetry of Europe, would apply themselves to learning the principal languages of Africa, and enter that great unexplored field of primitive song."

"There will soon, no doubt, be educated men of African descent who will be inspired with emulation, and will devote themselves to rendering this service to the mother-country."

"I am persuaded that the result would be the rescue of a store of mythological and historical poems of great interest. It is only a few years since Lönnrot enriched the world with a new epic which tradition had preserved among a people as little suspected of such wealth as the Africans now are."

"Have you ever known an African poet?"

"I have met with one who, though very young when he was made a slave, must, from his own account, have been already an esteemed bard in his country. I have heard him sing very agreeably in his native language; but he had acquired ours, and, being naturally desirous to be understood by his listeners, composed his poems in it. He had attained a skill in English versification which surprised me; but no man can make a foreign tongue completely his own. Some of his narrative poems, in which he forced the language to serve his ends, were spirited; but his more finished productions, such as hymns,— for which his talents were chiefly called into service,— were smooth and colorless. Yet he was a man of thought and judgment, and his mind had evidently had a certain training."

"Does it often happen that men of rank pass into foreign slavery?"

"It happens not unfrequently. And not only men of rank, but men of education, even according to our ideas of education, have shared the labors of the most abject slave on our plantations, and at last his grave. A few have been more fortunate, and have been restored to their country after some years' experience of slavery.

"About a century ago, the son of an African king was a slave in Maryland. His father, king of Bunda, had sent him to transact some business with an English captain, by name Pike, whose vessel was then lying in the Gambia. On his return, he was tempted by the desire of travelling. Dismissing his escort, he crossed the Gambia and entered a country that was hostile to his own. He was taken prisoner and carried before the king, who sold him to the same captain with whom he had himself had dealings. The captain, recognizing him, permitted him to write to his father for ransom, but set sail without waiting for the answer, and carried his prisoner to Maryland, where he was sold to a merchant of Annapolis. He succeeded in interesting his master in his story, and obtained permission to write to his father. His letter, which was written in Arabic, was sent to England to be given to Pike, who was to take it to Africa on his next voyage; it was seen by Oglethorpe, who sent it to Oxford to be translated, and, having thus learned the story of the unfortunate prince, sent him money to enable him to go to England. His case excited great sympathy there. He was presented at court, and treated with distinction. He was found to be very intelligent and well informed. He was much interested in everything he saw, and especially in the mechanism of instruments, which he understood without difficulty. Having once seen a clock taken to pieces, he put it together again without aid. His memory was extraordinary. He is described as a man of polished manners, — very agreeable in society, having a pleasant talent for narration; his conversation was marked by good sense and love of truth. He remained in England fourteen months, and was employed by Hans Sloane in translating Arabic manuscripts and inscriptions on medals. On his return to Africa, he found that the king who had sold him had accidentally shot himself with a pistol which there was reason to believe had been a part of the price received for him from the English captain. He thought he recognized the hand of Heaven both in this retribution, and in the mercy which, through the enlightenment he had gained in England, had turned an injury into a benefit."

"Have you ever met with a native African who appeared to have received anything like what we call education before coming to this country?"

"Many years ago,—indeed, it was when I was first making acquaintance with slavery and slaves,—I passed some time on the plantation of a distant relative of my father, in one of the older Southern States. He had an only son, a good, intelligent boy, but incapable of the sports and the studies of youth. His life was passed in almost constant suffering. His attendant was a native African who had received the name of Abel. This man was an object of great interest to me. He was sedate and silent; very faithful and very tender to his charge, but having always the air of one who offers protection, not service. He was stately to his fellow-slaves, who approached him with less assurance than they did their master. He used to draw the invalid in a small wagon, for hours every day, about the garden and grounds. I always made one of the strange party attendant on these promenades. I walked beside the wagon; on the other side went a tall black woman who had been the poor boy's nurse, and who always addressed him in the caressing tones used to infants. Behind came a troop of children and half-grown boys, who made a feint of being useful by rushing forward to lay hands on the wagon when a rivulet ran across the path or we approached a piece of uneven ground. These exhibitions of zeal were repressed by Abel before they passed into action; but they were uniformly renewed with the same fervor, on the next occasion. Abel suffered no one to aid but the nurse. Yet he did not banish the disorderly cortége. He was indulgent to their affection for their young master, when it was not too officious or too noisy.

"At a certain distance behind this rabble came a strange figure, — a small mulatto woman, in a costume more picturesque than harmonious or complete. Her great black eyes, which seemed to have outgrown her shrunk features, were fixed constantly on the little wagon, which she appeared to follow mechanically, as if drawn by some steady attraction. She was partially insane, but regarded as harmless. I learned that it was while left in this woman's charge for a short time by his nurse that the unfortunate child met with the accident which had ruined his life. Grief for the misfortune she had occasioned had, they told me, impaired her intellect. She was sent from the great house, and for some years employed to take care of the children of the plantation while their mothers were at work; but her disposition to wander becoming uncontrollable, she was exempted from all service. We always found her at a particular point of our road, standing on a high bank which overlooked it. When we had passed, she descended and followed. At first this wild figure fixed my attention strongly; but I soon became accustomed to its presence, and indifferent to it. Yet I observed, that, from time to time, Abel cast a sharp glance towards her. When sometimes the distance between her and the wagon was a little lessened, with a slight sign of his hand he made her retreat; and once, when, as we were winding along the edge of a deep ravine, she suddenly approached, as if about to offer aid, the words 'Too near!' in a stern voice, arrested her, and she remained standing motionless until the customary space separated her from the wagon.

"When the poor invalid sank into slumber, as he frequently did, we stopped in some pleasant spot. The escort then, dismissed by a wave of Abel's hand, disappeared into the woods, ready to start forth as soon as the wagon should be again in motion. Then the nurse would gather a branch from some tree or shrub, choosing, when she could, one loaded with blossoms, and seat herself on the ground beside the wagon. There, her head sunk on her breast, her eyes closed, she seemed to slumber from sympathy. Yet her care was wakeful. As long as the wagon halted, the fragrant fan waved backward and forward over it, with a slow, regular motion, keeping time with the breathing of the sleeper.

"I followed Abel, who commonly withdrew himself a little from the wagon, though not so far but that he could keep watch over it. He would sometimes remain long standing immovable, gazing intently forward, as if his soul were straining out into some distance greater than that the pine-wood before him bounded. This tall, silent figure seemed to my boyish imagination a personification of that vast, unexplored continent, land of mystery and marvel, of which nothing was known certainly but its sorrows. I desired ardently to know the history which had stamped that expression of resolute endurance on his proud, dark face. But I could not take advantage of my position to make an attempt on his confidence. It was long in giving itself to me. But a day came when suddenly, without premeditation, he opened his heart to me fully and simply, as one child to another. From that time his gloom seemed lightened. Those intervals of rest, which before were spent in mournful reverie, were now given to earnest conversation.

"Abel was a native of that mysterious Timbuctu whose very existence was so long called in question, and which was at that time known to the world only through the uncertain description of Leo Africanus and the romantic narratives of Adams and of Riley. Laing had not yet set out on his fatal expedition, and Caillé had not proved that it was possible for a European to see Timbuctu and live. You may imagine with what interest I listened to the recitals of Abel. He was the son of one of the principal officers of state, and had been carefully educated. He spoke and wrote Arabic, and gave me lessons in it, teaching me the letters by drawing them in the sand. He was well versed in the history of his country and the neighboring states. He told me of the rise and fall of dynasties, of ruined cities, once the seat of empire, but whose site is now marked only by crumbling walls inclosing a vast uncultivated space strewed with fragments of brick and pottery. He told me of the islands of rock, in the midst of their great plains, where the Swiss of Negroland had maintained an independence constantly threatened. As I followed his relations, and heard him refer to the annals he had studied, as to grave and authentic chronicles, it seemed to me I was listening to some strange parody of history. These remote, unknown states had their records of revolutions and counter-revolutions, of invasions successfully repelled, or a foreign yoke imposed. The rivalries and hates of royal families had given birth to tragedies as fearful as in Greece or England.

"The questions were not all on my side. He asked me concerning the government and laws of my country, its domestic customs, especially those of the States in which slavery is prohibited. His inquiries showed not only intelligence, but reflection, and a mind prepared to digest and classify information. I learned my own ignorance in regard to many important matters, through his interrogatories. He did not conceal from me his strong desire to recover his liberty, or rather, his fixed determination to do so in one way or another. He had considered all the chances of escape; but his great intelligence made him fully acquainted with the difficulties that surrounded an attempt at flight. He knew that such an attempt and failure would greatly lessen his chances of success by another scheme. He had not the hardihood of the ignorant slave, which carries him safely through perils he would not have risked, if he had understood them. Another feeling still held Abel where he was: attachment to the boy under his care. 'How can I leave him,' he said, anxiously, 'until he is strong enough to do without me, or'—— He could not speak the alternative. 'He needs to be watched over.' As he said this, he cast around him a keen glance, which rested searchingly on a cluster of trees from behind one of which I thought I saw the flutter of drapery, but, as I looked, it had disappeared. 'He needs to be watched over,' Abel repeated,—'only I know how closely.'"

"Had he any special meaning?"

"He did not explain himself; and it was not until many years afterwards—after the death of the poor boy, and the departure of Abel—that I understood his words, and learned that he had penetrated what was a secret to every one else."

"The crazy woman!"

"Yes. It was one of those terrible instances of servile vengeance which from time to time startle the master out of his security, but which are soon forgotten again, until a new tragedy of the same kind calls to mind the old one."

"Did she reveal her crime herself?"

"On her deathbed, which was watched by the mistress whose house she had made desolate. She revealed it, not in penitence, but in a last moment of triumph."

"So the boy died! And Abel escaped?"

"No; his master was just to him. The suffering child expressed, a few months before his death, in the presence of his father, — a proud, generous man, — his warm gratitude to his faithful attendant. 'But, oh, Abel,' he said, 'if I could only think you took care of me for love, and not because you must!' — 'I have served you from choice,' Abel answered; 'have I ever called you master?' — And the father: 'I cannot suffer a slave to speak thus in my presence. Abel, you are a free man.'

"When his duties were ended by the death of his charge, Abel entered the service of an Englishman who was travelling in this country, and went with him to England. I wrote to his former master, a few months after, to ask information concerning him. I learned that a letter had been received, announcing his safe arrival. In this letter was inclosed one for me; but it had unfortunately been mislaid. He had sent his address; it had also been lost and forgotten."

A heavy tread approached the door; a broad face intruded, — a face that might have been the impersonation of Duty, so honest, so insensible, so obstinate. Edward received the summons as coming from that determined divinity, and offered no resistance.

V.

The evening came and brought back my friend. Though I had claimed so much of his time during the day, I did not scruple to call for the expected reading. It was less interrupted by conversation than usual. As I have already said, Colvil talked with me of his personages as if they had been real existences, frequently adding details in regard to their character or history, and accepting or rejecting frankly the strictures I made on his delineation. This was the case with all but his heroine, to whom this evening introduced me. He did not seem inclined to talk of her, but left me to what was written. Sometimes, at a question or remark I made concerning her, he turned back to the passage that called it forth and read it again to himself, with the expression a painter has, when, the comment of a passer-by suggesting an unwilling doubt, he eyes his work distrustfully with suspended pencil. Edward did not give me the result of his scrutiny; but I observed afterwards insertions and alterations in the manuscript, some of which I thought had been suggested by a query or comment of mine.

Day followed day to find me still an inmate of the remote farm-house, the charm still unbroken, the outpouring of thoughts and confidences still unexhausted. But my satisfaction, in this life of freedom from conventionalities and in this new pleasure of unconstrained friendship, was troubled by an occasional prick of conscience, which reminded me that I was prolonging too much the vacation allowed me by my father, and that he might already be uneasy at my absence from the counting-room, where I was useless, but where it was his pleasure that I should pass a certain number of hours every day. The state of his health made a small matter important to him, and did not permit me to hazard his suffering any anxiety, however unreasonable. My convalescence had received no check. I could find no pretext for a further delay. I rose one morning decided that the next day should see me on my road towards the North.

I had now for several days successively made myself Edward's companion when he went out to his work. On this morning he proposed to me that we should walk together over his whole farm, whose entire beauties and resources he had not yet displayed to me. I resolved to take this occasion to set forth the projects with which I had been pleasing myself. I had arranged everything satisfactorily in my own mind. Edward was to forward to me a copy of each of his finished works, and I was at once to take measures for having them brought before the public. I had considered my plans maturely, had called up all objections, and prepared myself to refute them.

Colvil's estate offered little variety, and to me little interest, except what it gained from being his. I should have felt a profound pity for my farmer friend, if he had seemed at all to stand in need of it. But the cheerful glance with which he scanned his little domain, the satisfaction with which he spoke of his future crops and his plans for increasing them, the animated pleasure with which he called my attention to beauties in his landscape which I should not have thought of looking for, and hardly found when he pointed them out, forbade me to regard him as an object of compassion.

I had not yet told Edward that this day was to be my last with him. A deep shade passed over his face when I made this announcement, which I did abruptly, for it cost me an effort. He began to offer remonstrances; but the plea of duty instantly checked them. I could see, however, that he was disappointed and saddened. His eye moved listlessly over the landscape which had brightened it but a few moments before. I was not so selfish as to rejoice in this proof of the consequence I was to him. I felt that my departure would leave a blank in his life, greater perhaps than the separation from him would make in mine. To me this friendship was the crowning wreath to a full cup; to him was it not as the single flower that had sprung up in the waste? I hastened to lay before him the project which was to form a link between us and give us a subject of interest in common.

The recipient of a confidence like that I had been intrusted with stands somewhat in the same relation to the work of his friend that a bachelor uncle does to his brother's son. His expectations are commonly more unreasonable than those of the real parent; if they are in any degree fulfilled, he has his full share of satisfaction; if they are defeated, he has a mild disappointment which he is at least at liberty to think unmerited. He is very courageous, then, the self-elected sponsor of an inedited book; he has something to look forward to, and not much at risk.

I entered on the detail of my plans with a zeal so little restrained, that Edward could not help regarding me with an amused smile, which only led me to combat more earnestly the dissent I thought it implied. I exhausted myself in arguments and assurances before I gave him an opportunity to reply. He yielded half my demand, and postponed his answer to the other half. He gave me a willing promise to send me a copy of his finished dramas, and also to complete for me those that were only begun.

"It will enhance the pleasure of writing," he said, "to know that I am writing for you; and the necessity of giving you the end of a story of which you have had the beginning will prevent me from letting myself be seduced by a new subject before the old one has been worked out."

As to the rest of my scheme, he thought it was to be maturely considered before it was adopted.

"We have time before us. You are public enough for me at present."

I could not move him from this point. But I was, on the whole, satisfied with what I had secured. I had not hoped to gain so much thus easily. It was a proof, very precious to me, of his confidence in my affection, that he should willingly, even gladly, give over to my inspection productions of whose value he was not himself assured.

The moment of parting came. "You will not forget me?" I said, as I held out my hand to Edward for the last time. A firm, slowly tightening pressure was the only answer. I felt in it the assurance of a constant, only deepening affection.

I was returning to my father's house, — a house with which were associated ideas of refined luxury combined with order not excessive, a wise liberality, and the decorum of high breeding. Nor was kindness wanting there, true and steadfast. Why was it, that, when the gate, which had opened to me for the first time only three weeks before, closed behind me, I felt as if excluded from a home?

I did not look back, but I held my horse in to a walk until I knew the house was no longer in sight. Every step he planted in the sand seemed like a seal set on my sentence of banishment.

My sadness did not last, however unwilling I was to part with it. The fresh air of the morning and the lively step of my horse, who was with difficulty restrained to a pace that suited my reluctance, had, in spite of me, their effect on my youthful constitution. I gradually yielded myself to the exhilarating influences. The last traces of my melancholy were dissipated, when, in the afternoon, I came into a higher region, where the air was more bracing, the prospect wide and varied. I began to look out cheerily into the world. I thought with pleasure of the old scenes to which I was going back enriched. Every object which rose up before my mind seemed, like myself, to have had something added to its life. There was waiting for me the room I had so minutely described to Colvil. I had drawn for him the tree whose branches sweep its windows. There on my shelves were books of which I had talked with him; others that had had their day of favor, but were now to give place to new friends he had taught me to love. In my secretary were drawers destined to receive his manuscripts.

And my father,—how venerable his figure rose before me! how precious seemed his simple, dignified affection! My stately, silent sister,—I felt a pride in her beauty, her womanly worth. I looked forward with pleasure even to seeing the common acquaintances who I had sometimes thought bored me. I believed I should find their conversation no longer so vapid as before. The society of ordinary acquaintances is, to him who has a friend, like the dessert after a dinner; but he who has no deeper affection, for a stand-by, can no more satisfy himself with it than a hungry man with comfiture.

The reality fell no farther short of anticipation than it always does. In my father's greeting there was a shade of sadness, due to my lengthened absence. It was slight, and vanished as soon as he saw I had perceived it; but the interview was not as I had rehearsed it beforehand. I went to my sister. I found her preoccupied by some pressing cares of her own, and my return moved her less than I had expected.

In the evening I joined the family circle with lower expectations. Their humility was rewarded. My father seemed to have gained health by my arrival. He hardly looked infirm, as he sat erect in his arm-chair. His eye beamed affectionately on me, as I entered. He received with his natural urbanity the friends who came in to welcome me on my return. He spoke little, — but took part in the conversation, which was animated and genial, by his ready smile and appreciating gesture. My sister was charming, — as she was when some occasional excitement took her out of her habitual calm. I knew it was my return that brightened her look and gave vivacity to her thoughts, and I was grateful. I wrote to Colvil that night, and talked to him of my home as I had dreamed it, and as I had already described it to him.

I was impatient to carry out my plans. Books, now, had a new form of interest for me. I became a critic in paper and print. I examined the external qualities of new publications, discovered merits and demerits to which I had been blind, and learned to distinguish shades of difference which had hitherto escaped me. I had soon fixed on the form, the size of the type, the quality of the paper. I delayed, however, to engage a publisher until I should have the complete work in my hands.

The precaution proved not to have been superfluous. Colvil's first letter brought me a disappointment. In reply to my urgent demands for the manuscripts, he begged me to forgive him, if he made me wait a little. He must make some corrections and insertions before sending them, and could not then command the necessary leisure. His farm duties occupied not only almost every hour, but almost every thought. In the intervals of rest he was too much fatigued for anything but desultory reading. He asked me to send him such extracts from my journal as might enable him to follow in some measure my daily life, and offered to keep one for me in return.

"I shall have no more important events to record for you," he wrote, "than the arrival of a new book, or the reading of an old one in a new light, — the passage of a party of emigrants, or perhaps the rare visit of a traveller whom the love of exploring has drawn aside from the great high-road. But whatever my life offers you shall have a part in. Let me share in yours."

I accepted this proposal gladly. His journal was not very full at first, but it gradually expanded. He took up the habit of sending me notes on the books he was reading, and sometimes gave me a complete analysis of them. He often recurred to the subject of our former discussions, — giving me new illustrations of African character, and new facts, or the testimony of new authorities, in confirmation of the views he had supported.

"When we were reading over," he wrote, "the evening before you went away, your notes of our conversations upon Africa, I marked several passages to which I meant to add a further explanation; but there was so much left to do and say, in our last hours together, that I neglected it.

"I ought to have told you, that Bowdich, when he made that terrible statement in regard to the perfidy of English captains to whom the native princes and nobles had intrusted their children, acquits the French of this infamy. Their promises of this kind, he says, have always been redeemed. He saw several men, sons of chiefs, who had been educated in France. One of them had been committed to an English captain, whose vessel was captured by a French privateer before he had had time to make an exception to the general villany of his class or to load himself with a new crime. The French captain carried the boy to France, and the owner of the privateer fulfilled the engagement thus transferred to him: he had the boy carefully educated, and sent him back to his own country. It will not do to pass over an instance of honorable conduct on the part of a white man towards a black man; there are not too many such to record.

" On the subject of slavery among the Africans I will add a few particulars which I believe I forgot to give you. The law which, in Africa, prohibits the sale of domestic slaves admits of certain exceptions: in time of famine the master is permitted to sell one of his slaves in order to buy food; and the insolvency of the master subjects the slave to seizure. The bankrupt-laws of Africa are severe. The debtor, even if a man of rank and consequence, must himself become the slave of the creditor whom he has no other means of satisfying. If this creditor be a foreign trader, the doom is indeed appalling; but if he be an African, passing into his employment does not necessarily imply any greater change of condition than often follows loss of fortune in other countries. Domestic service in Africa does not inspire any peculiar dread. It is not uncommon, when a family is in pecuniary embarrassment, for one member of it to devote himself to servitude for the benefit of the rest. The family receives a certain sum of money on his account, and he remains in the service of the person who advances it until it is repaid. It is incumbent on his family to release him as soon as possible. It is also a point of honor with the master whose domestic slave has been seized for his debts to redeem him when it is in his power. But, again, when the claimant is a foreigner, even the integrity and affection of the master can afford the poor victim no hope.

"I believe the cases I have mentioned are the only ones in which an African domestic, not convicted of crime, can be legally sold. The master is not himself the judge of an accused slave; he cannot sell him for any offence without 'calling a palaver on his conduct,' or, in other words, 'bringing him to a public trial.' This appears to be the common law of Negro Africa, for it is reported by different travellers as existing in different regions. Is not this continued recognition of laws restricting the power of the master over the slave enough in itself to show us the falseness of our prevailing notions in regard to native African civilization? Can we refuse to admire the rectitude and stability of the negro character which has thus maintained the ancient institutions of the country, assailed and undermined as they have been for centuries by every form of violence and temptation? Without doubt, the force of the laws for the protection of the slave has been weakened by the demoralization caused by the foreign slave-trade; without doubt, they have been often evaded, sometimes disregarded; but they are still acknowledged by the general conscience, and upheld by public opinion. The man who violates them incurs the danger of disgrace; and in no country are the claims of honor more imperative than in Africa. The 'spoiling of a man's name' is the greatest injury that can be inflicted on him.

"The natural religion of the African furnishes another protection to the slave, as well against cruel treatment as unlawful sale. It is believed that the imprecation of the injured man has power to bring down a judgment from Heaven. It is common for travellers to speak of this fear as a childish superstition. But is it not, in truth, the fear of God? Are not we also taught to believe that the voice of a brother's blood will cry unto Him from the ground?

"There are travellers who see in the country they visit only what they expected to see, and go away with precisely the same impressions they brought with them. It must be that the greater part of readers go through books of travel in the same manner, retaining only what fits in comfortably with old prejudices. There is no other way of accounting for the hold that certain errors in regard to Africa have on the public mind. We constantly hear it said, and even by persons who are not friends to slavery, as it exists here, that it is an immense gain for negro Africans and their descendants to be in the service of civilized men, rather than, as they might have been, at the mercy of Pagan monsters. Yet all the world has read the statements which travellers of the highest reputation have made in regard to the character of slavery in Africa, and the laws which regulate it.

"The slavery of African to African is, in truth, the mildest form of serfdom. It is not unusual for the slave to call the master 'My father.' The name by which his condition is denoted has not for him the meaning which we attach to the word 'slave'; for it implies neither degradation nor hopelessness. If he possess more than common abilities, these are allowed free scope. The slave is sometimes a richer man than his master; he can even attain to high office in the state, if his talents and his tastes lead him in that direction. If he remain a humble husbandman, or artisan, or household-servant, his duties are light, and he has no fear of being crushed either by severity or contempt.

"The American planter owes, I believe, more than he is aware to the view of the relation of master and slave which his negro has inherited from Africa. The unquestioning acquiescence of the slave in his lot, his absorption in the family on which he depends, and identification of its interests with his own, are parts of a very old creed. The self-devotion, which has more of the spirit of clanship than of servility, and which the master himself must love and wonder at, is traditional. It dates from a time when the relation of superior and dependant was endeared by the sense of a common blood and a common country. It does not belong to a temporary and uncertain connection. Yet these principles of fidelity and trust are so deeply implanted in the heart of the African that they are capable of sustaining very rude shocks. Where they have been met by anything like a corresponding sense of duty on the part of the master, above all, where they have been fostered by a true Christian love, they have even struck new and deeper roots. The most unworthy master has still his share of the old traditional affection. The African slave, even after long experience of hardship, is reluctant to believe any unmerited privation or severity which he endures is inflicted by his master. He prefers to give the blame to a subordinate. Even when his master is the direct agent, he willingly supposes him to have been misinformed or misled by another. On the remote plantation, where the despotism of the overseer is unrestricted, the slaves often cling to the belief, that, if their wrongs could come to the master's knowledge, everything would be set right. I have known this illusion maintained under circumstances which made it seem almost miraculous.

" The African slave in America has not only a transmitted loyalty, but likewise an inherited sense of rights and privileges. Many of those perverse notions in regard to right and wrong, which, as the phrase is, 'cannot be got out of his head,' are fragments of the ancient African code. As he expects to suffer for the reverses of his superiors, so he believes he has a prescriptive right to ease and plenty in their prosperity; he imagines himself to have a certain property in the property of his master, and thinks he can take some liberties with it, especially in the articles of meat and drink, without subjecting himself to the disgrace of dishonesty. Above all, he is firm in the belief that the sale of an innocent man is unjust and unlawful. Such an act, on the part of his master, is a stretch of authority which he cannot be made to comprehend, and which he does not submit to without remonstrance, except when he has been brought to the last stage of apathy, or when hopelessness gives him the last degree of self-control. When a great calamity involves the master and his dependants in the same ruin, they accept the sentence of separation as the decree of Fate, and grieve for him even more than for themselves; but in other cases they protest, openly or secretly. Whatever outward appearance there may be of submission, the mother never consents to the sale of her children; never forgets it; her forgiveness, if she forgive, is a sacrifice made to her Heavenly Master; the service she thenceforth performs is not so much a duty rendered as a charity offered for the love of God. Too often she interweaves with her daily toil the black thread which, in the land of her ancestors, she would have had power to work into the web of her master's fate, but which here can probably only deepen the darkness of her own. Such is not, however, the belief of our Africans; in their faith, the malediction of the wronged has still its old power.

"Not only the prejudices and superstitions of the Africans, but also some of their peculiar virtues have clung to them in their exile. They are still 'very charitable,' as Ca da Mosto described them not many years after they were discovered by the Portuguese; they are still 'gentle and loving,' as Welsh found them a century later; they are tender to children; their filial piety — a virtue nowhere carried farther than in Africa — is admirable.

"What painful questions we are forced to ask ourselves, when we see the constancy of these traits in the negro! Have his native qualities been fostered by us and developed into higher and more enlightened virtues? Is the mother aided to train up her son to truth and courage by the hope of rejoicing in his noble manhood? Is the son strengthened in virtue by the ambition of becoming the prop and pride of his father's old age? Are not these dear affections often for this kindly people the source of the keenest sorrows and anxieties our nature can know?

"What have the African serfs and their descendants gained in exchanging a Pagan patron for a Christian master? A certain number of them have gained what they would not barter for ease and enjoyment. Those who, in their captivity, have 'received the spirit of adoption whereby they cry Abba, Father,' no longer rely on an earthly protection. But was the ruin of those millions necessary to the redemption of these hundreds? Must we think so basely of our own race as to believe that it demands this fearful compensation for imparting that which it has itself obtained without money and without price?

"A few words more in regard to the charge of cannibalism which is so often brought up against Africa. I gave you Robertson's opinion on this subject, and Tuckey's. I might have told you that this charge was contradicted, more than a century ago, by Doctor Atkins, a surgeon in the British navy, an intelligent and well-educated man. He took some pains to inquire into the evidence on this point, and satisfied himself that the worst anthropophagi in Africa were the mosquitoes. He found that injurious reports often had their origin in the fears of the European sailors, who had the habit of giving a reputation for man-eating to places which they wished to avoid, because they had reason to dread the vengeance of the inhabitants. In some instances, the cruelty and treachery of the Europeans had provoked reprisals on the part of the natives, and this had furnished quite sufficient ground for a charge of cannibalism. The inhabitants of Cape Saint Mary, who then lay under this accusation, proved, he says, to be a gentle and civil people, who supplied them with firewood for their vessel.

" A suspicion of dreadful practices has sometimes been suggested by incidents or expressions which, when examined into, are not found to imply anything very atrocious. It is easy to misapprehend the usages and figures of speech of a people whose manners and language are so utterly foreign to the observer.

" Among the kind civilities offered by the king of the Fulahs to Brüe, Director of the Senegal Company, Labat mentions this singular attention: 'The king sent him a young slave for his supper.' Happily, the explanation is immediately given: 'It is not to be supposed this young man was boiled or roasted; he was alive and well. It was a galanterie the king made to the general; he simply wished to let him know that the slave was sent as a pure gift. For, inasmuch as what is eaten is not paid for, it would be discourtesy to accept a return for what has been given under the name of food.' Imagine a traveller as yet unversed in the terms of African politeness receiving a galanterie of this sort on his first presentation at court!

"The custom, which exists in some parts of Africa, of exposing the bodies of malefactors, has sometimes led travellers to give credit to reports of cannibalism. It must be unpleasant to a civilized man to come unexpectedly on a heap of human bones, or a suspended skeleton. No wonder such a spectacle excites strange fears. But we must remember that it is only very lately that Europeans have had a right to be astonished at it. It was not an African, but an English mother, who, going to her work, left her children under the gallows where her husband's body was hanging, 'to play in the care of their father.'

"It has been urged that African nations have accused each other of cannibalism. So have European. Mr. James Lancaster, captain of a tall ship which took him to Zanzibar in 1591, was informed by the people there of the 'false and spiteful dealing of the Portugals, which made them believe that we were cruel people and men-eaters, and willed them, if they loved their safetie, in no case to come neere us. This they did to cut us off from all knowledge of the state and traffique of the country.'

"Certain expressions in the war-songs of some African peoples have been received as proof of the presence of cannibals among them. There is as good or better evidence that Richard the First of England supped on a Saracen. The minstrel who records this feast makes Richard boast, —

"'We shall never die for default,
While we may in any assault
Slee Saracens, the flesh may take,
And seethen and rosten and do hem bake.
With one Saracen I may feed
Well a nine or a ten
Of my good Christian men.
King Richard shall warrant
There is no flesh so nourissant
Unto an English man,
Partridge, plover, heron ne swan,
Cow ne ox, sheep ne swine,
As the head of a Sarazyn.
There he is, fat and thereto tender,
And my men be lean and slender.
While any Saracen quick be
Livand now in this Syrie,
For meat will we nothing care;
Abouten fast we shall fare,
And every day we shall eat
All so many as we may get.
To England will we nought gon
Till they be eaten every one.'

"I doubt whether African minstrelsy, ancient or modern, can furnish anything much more to the purpose than this.

"I want to engage you to read accounts of Africa in the same spirit in which you read accounts of other countries, — to divest yourself of the feeling that its inhabitants are not of a like nature with ourselves. And do not accept blindly whatever your author gives you. Take into consideration, as you would in other cases, his character, his education, and especially his prejudices, whether of nationality or station or profession. We have need here of a more than common candor and caution. In forming our judgments of other countries, we have access to a vast amount and variety of testimony, their own not being excluded. But Africa is not yet capable of speaking for herself, or, at least, we are not yet capable of listening to her.

"It is surprising how little resemblance there is between a people's own sketches of itself and its portrait as drawn by a stranger.

"Read this account of a people whom Careri, the Italian traveller, visited in 1686: —

"'The commonalty are rude and cruel, addicted to thieving and robbing, faithless, headstrong, inclined to strife and mutiny, gluttonous, and superstitiously addicted to the predictions of foolish astrologers; in short, of a very extravagant temper, delighting in the noise of guns, drums, and bells, as if it were some sweet harmony. . . . As for drunkenness, they delight in it so much, that, though they own it to be a great fault in their nation, yet they never endeavor to refrain.'

"What unpleasant barbarians are these? They are a people inhabiting the southern part of an island lying west of the continent of Europe. They are called the English people.

"Careri relates, further, that they have a great taste for 'playing the pirate': 'They are so fond of this infamous gain, that many sell all they have to buy a ship and set out a-robbing.'

"They are so courageous, and despise death so madly, that Careri infers, 'They can have no good notion of the immortality of the soul, the knowledge whereof causes strong apprehension even in the bravest souls.'

"It is not only on the battle-field that they show their contempt of death: 'You may see a man condemned to be hanged go to the gallows as if it were to a wedding, and his nearest kindred pull him by the heels with the greatest indifference in the world.'

"The men of superior condition seem, if more refined than the commonalty, to be, in their way, almost as unamiable: 'The gentry are courteous and generous to strangers, and, to say the truth, vie with the French in this particular; but they are not so open-hearted, nor their countenances so affable and affectionate to others; for they rather appear proud and haughty than otherwise. What I much admire is, that, if a man converses with them modestly and humbly, they do not look upon it as civility and good-breeding, but as meanness of spirit, and therefore they undervalue him, though they would have all to submit to them. They are fond of titles and other marks of honor, and oblige their many servants to attend them in very servile manner.'

"Careri allows this people all the merit he can. Although it might reasonably be inferred, he says, from their excessive eating and drinking, that they are stupid and dull, yet it is quite otherwise: 'For, besides their being extraordinary sharp traders, they improve wonderfully in all sciences whatsoever; so that Nature seems to have given them this to balance all their vices.'

"Careri's opinion of the England of the seventeenth century will not, probably, have much influence on yours. For this England is your England. Your own ancestors were, perhaps, among those gentlemen whose manly bearing he mistook for haughtiness, or those stout yeomen whose robust appetite he stigmatized as gluttony. You know that religious faith aided the British soldier to meet death so dauntlessly; it was the true old English pluck, found even in thieves, that made those condemned men go to the gallows as to a wedding.

"For you, Careri's sketch has just enough of truth to make it delightfully absurd; but by the greater part of his readers on the continent of Europe it was, no doubt, accepted as accurate. And they had much reason to confide in him as an authority. He was a man of capacity, education, and fortune, travelling solely for his own pleasure and instruction. His account of England was originally written in letters to an intimate friend. He had every motive for being impartial and exact: no doubt, he believed himself to have been so. His other travels were highly esteemed, in their day, by the English themselves: I do not know how satisfactory they may have been to the peoples described in them.

"It is not enough that a traveller is sincere, intelligent, and cultivated. To be a good observer of men, he must likewise possess a great power of sympathy; otherwise, seeing, he will not perceive; and what he misses may be precisely what is most characteristic. Travellers in Africa have more than usual need to be largely endowed with this gift.

"Do not think I want to persuade you to like everything in Africa. I only want you to have your eyes open to the good as to the bad. Africa has its fair side, as the most privileged lands have their dark one. Let us not take for granted, because some wretched sea-port or river-station, for centuries a den of men-thieves, is found pestilent with moral and physical disease, that this condemned spot is an epitome of Africa. I do not call in question the accuracy of the descriptions travellers give us of such places as Badagry, Brass, Bonny Town, and the rest; nor do I ask you to feel anything but horror of them. I give you leave to dislike base manners and deadly climate wherever they are found. I shall not expect you, for example, to envy travelling-experiences like the following, or to feel a desire to emigrate to the country which was the scene of them: —

" 'The inn at which we lodged was the best in the town, and yet was such a disgusting place that it was a punishment to live in it. Everything was filthy. Putrid water was served in dirty vessels. Swarms of flies settled on the meats, which were seasoned with rancid oil. During the day we were harassed by mosquitoes and gnats from the marshes, which covered us with their painful stings, and at night we were devoured by other insects, equally tormenting and far more disgusting.

" 'Fever and death are brought into the town by putrid miasmata from the fens and lagoons. . . . It is especially in the month of August that the fever rages. During that month, the sound of the funeral-bell is heard incessantly. A young man who waited on us had lost, in a single day, his grandmother, mother, and aunt. . . . The livid complexions, hollow cheeks, and sunken eyes of men whom we met in the streets made us feel as if we were within the inclosure of a great hospital whose patients had obtained permission to take a walk.'

"Am I reading of 'The White Man's Grave'? you ask, perhaps. No: of La belle France,—of that part of it which is most rich in historical and poetical associations. You have been reading of Provence. The wretched town which can offer only putrid water to its guests attracts them by the remains of magnificent aqueducts. The marshes and ponds which sicken it with noxious exhalations occupy the place of the fine port which received three hundred vessels after the Battle of Actium. It is Fréjus, the ancient Forum Julii, the birthplace of Agricola. No prejudiced foreigner drew that dismal picture, but a patriotic Frenchman, who was preparing for more distant travel by making himself acquainted with his own country,—M. Millin, a member of the Institute, and already at that time (1805) one of the most distinguished scholars of France.

"It is possible thus to retrograde in the very heart of civilization. The region so blighted by infection is, according to M. Millin, the most fertile in Provence,—'a true land of promise.' 'The inhabitants,' he says, 'do nothing to avert the evils by which they are assailed; they seem to be waiting for a miracle from Providence.'

"'How humiliated ought the people of this country to be,'—I am still quoting M. Millin,—'having always before their eyes the remains of the great works of the Romans! These masters of the world, recognizing the advantages possessed by Fréjus, in its mild climate and happy situation, resolved to found a great establishment there. They erected a mole to protect the port, spacious magazines to hold provisions, a vast aqueduct to bring in pure water, large reservoirs to receive it. The inhabitants of a place otherwise so favored by Nature have let these fine constructions perish: it would have been easy to restore the canals built by the Romans; a premature death has carried off in ten years more people than would have been sufficient to execute these works; and yet no one has thought of proposing such an undertaking.'

"Fréjus is not the only city of Provence condemned to breathe poisoned air and drink tainted water. In many other towns of that beautiful country, the same neglect is visited by the same penalty.

"And how is it with the character of the men in the land of romance? Indolent it would seem they must be. Is their supineness compensated by their easy temper and frank kind-heartedness?

12

This is what M. Millin has to say of them: his is not precisely the ideal Provençal peasant: —

" 'The Provençal peasants, in general, are not to be confided in. Those of the neighborhood of Toulon are particularly ill-natured. If you inquire your way of them, they do not answer, or answer only to mislead you. Be sure that all is right with your carriage and harness, for you need look for no assistance from them. If they see you in difficulty, they laugh; if you are in danger, they pass on. If a thirsty traveller should gather a bunch of grapes, he may think himself fortunate, if this slight indiscretion do not draw upon him a blow with a stick or a shot from a musket. Their cries are those of a tiger; their vivacity is that of rage. Quarrels arise on the slightest occasion. They begin with abuse: this is answered by a blow with a stick, or a thrust with a knife, which often proves mortal. He who has committed the crime, on becoming cool, does not think of its atrocity, but of its consequences. He abandons his victim, whom he might aid, or despatches him in order to be safe from his testimony. He then takes refuge in the valleys of Olioulles or in the woods of Esterel, and lies in wait for the traveller, — beginning with robbery, and ending an assassin by profession.'

" M. Millin's travels were widely read in foreign

countries; but it does not appear that France has been shunned on account of its malignant climate and savage people.

"It has not been suggested, I believe, that it would be wholesome for the Provençal peasant to be transported into foreign servitude and taught to be useful, or at least harmless. We know, in part, the causes that have been at work to render him distrustful, resentful, and rebellious. We can feel that this proud, independent, impetuous character may have its interesting side. We are glad to know that its harsher features have already softened, and we trust that its finer traits may find full opportunity of development.

"Let us be hopeful for the African. At least, inhospitality and ferocity are not his chief characteristics.

"Let us be hopeful; but, at the same time, let us not expect too much; and especially, let us not make up our minds too exactly as to what we ought to expect, even of colonies founded under Anglo-Saxon auspices and endowed with Anglo-Saxon institutions, lest disappointment should again make us unjust. Young nations, like young persons, often shock the judgment and wound the taste of their elders. And then, all the world assumes the right to criticize and admonish. The citizen of a long-established state, who does one of these upstarts the honor of visiting it, to inspect its progress, looks down upon it from the height of his national dignity, and writes of it condescendingly or scornfully, according to his temper. In either case, all its little weaknesses are sure to be fully reported. We have passed through this ordeal. I need not say how peculiarly exposed the rising states of Africa are to be made the subjects of scrutiny and animadversion. Knowing what the way of the world is in this respect, we ought not to allow ourselves to be too much impressed by unfavorable reports. It should not surprise or dishearten the friends of free institutions to meet with such an account as this of the Representative Assembly of a young republic: —

"'Attending the debates on a day when a subject of consequence was to be discussed, I left the House full of contempt for its eloquence and the paucity of talent employed for the support or consideration of the question. Notwithstanding this, I read in the next morning's gazette that "a debate took place in the House last night of the most interesting nature, and that it was agitated by all the talent of the country, — particularly by Messrs. ——— and ———, whose brilliant speeches we lay before the public." Here followed certainly eloquent orations, a sentence of which never passed in the House. . . . The Congress is a violent, vulgar assembly, and the public newspapers are conducted by foreign editors, who amplify such debates and give them something of a polished and interesting character.'

"Is this an account of the Congress of Liberia? It is an account of the Congress of the United States in 1806, given by an English traveller, — Thomas Ashe, Esquire, — who in that year visited 'the civilized parts' of America, and went home with a great respect for the natural resources of the country and a great contempt for its inhabitants. 'Alas!' he exclaims, after expatiating on the 'riches yielded by its soil,' 'it may be said with the greatest truth, — "Man is the only growth that dwindles here."'

"Ashe's observations on the United States, like Careri's on England, were written in the form of letters to a friend. 'His researches cannot fail,' according to one of his countrymen, 'to interest and inform the politician, the statesman, the philosopher, and the antiquary.' One of his greatest merits, it seems, was that he exposed 'the delusions that have been held up by fanciful or partial writers as to the country, by which so many individuals have been misled.' It certainly was not Mr. Ashe's fault, if any of his countrymen continued to be misled by delusions favorable to the United States, or the political principles in vogue there, — principles which, in his opinion, 'are not only adverse to the enjoyment of practical liberty, and to the existence of regular authority, but destructive also of comfort and security in every class of society.'

"Mr. Ashe's first letter is from Pittsburg, Pennsylvania. He does not write from the Northern States, because they are 'unworthy the observation' of his correspondent. 'The Middle States are less contemptible. They produce grain for exportation. . . . The national features here are not strong, and those of different emigrants have not yet composed a face of local deformity.' He even finds some tolerable society at Pittsburg. The influence of a number of Irish families who had settled there 'had been favorable to the town,' and had 'hindered the vicious propensities of the genuine American character from establishing here the horrid dominion which they have assumed over the Atlantic States.'

"I have told you what Mr. Ashe thought of our public men of that time. 'The Church,' he found, had 'no brighter ornaments than the State.' He went to hear a preacher who had 'the highest reputation as a divine and orator, and had the mortification to hear a transposed sermon of Blair, delivered in a strain of dull monotony.' As for the law, he was 'not surprised to find a want of ability and eloquence in that department.' It was worse still with medicine. ‘There is no profession in America so shamefully neglected as that of physic, or more destitute of able practitioners.’

“I must be just to Mr. Ashe, and tell you that he approves of the women of the United States. ‘It gives me great pleasure,’ he tells his friend, ‘to assure you, that, when I expressed the supreme disgust excited in me by the people of the United States, the ladies were by no means included in the general censure.’

“The deterioration of the men of the United States seems, in Mr. Ashe's view, to be chiefly attributable to political doctrines prevalent in that country, — doctrines whose tendency is, according to him, ‘to make men turbulent citizens, abandoned Christians, inconstant husbands, and treacherous friends.’

“Political prepossessions could thus limit the sympathies and warp the judgment of an Englishman travelling among a kindred people. What allowance, in reading foreign accounts of Africa, ought we not to make for the influence of that most fatal prejudice of race!

“It was from books like Mr. Ashe's that the English used to form their opinion of the people of the United States; so that, when they saw a well-bred American, they took him for an exception, and told him he might almost pass for an Englishman. I do not know that we ever lost anything in our own esteem through the portraits drawn of us by the English, any more than those stout islanders have thought the worse of themselves for what was said of them on the Continent.

"This innate sense of worth is not confined to nations who have so undoubted a right to it as we and our cousins of England. It is pleasant to know that the least-considered peoples have as comfortable a sense of superiority as the most eminent. When Carr — 'The Stranger in Ireland' — was passing through the magnificent scenery in the neighborhood of Killarney, his Irish driver turned to him with, 'Ah, your Honor, here are glens and mountains! If you had those in your country, what a fine thing it would be for the robbers and murderers there! By my shoul, they are here of no use!' Carr's English pride did not wholly defend him from mortification. He took some pains to explain that England 'had glens and mountains not infested by robbers and murderers.' But the Irishman only shook his head incredulously. 'I found in many parts of Ireland,' adds Mr. Carr, 'the same unfortunate and unpleasant prejudice.'

"The Anglo-Saxon becomes sensitive even to African opinion, when he finds himself alone with it. In truth, it is startling to see how completely the tables are turned upon the white man in the country of the blacks. Wherever he goes, he is obliged, in a manner, to apologize for his skin. For the natives are not only insensible to its beauty, but they actually have a notion that the faded hue is the sign of an impoverished stock and argues a lack of the higher moral qualities. In fact, the white man has to earn a reputation for himself by respectable conduct, before the testimony borne against him by his complexion can be disallowed.

"When a white man shows himself, for the first time, unexpectedly in an African village, the women run, screaming, to hide their children. After the inoffensiveness of the stranger has been established by his quiet demeanor and the testimony of his black attendants, the people begin to approach, look at him with wonder, venture at last to touch his hair gently, and then report to those who have not yet dared to come so near, — 'It is not a man; it has a mane!' The greatest compliment that can be paid to a white man who has given proof of his intrinsic good qualities is to tell him that he 'deserves to be black.'

"It is in the countries in which Mahometanism has established itself that the white color is seen with the most distrust, because it is associated with the Christians, 'the men who never pray and who eat swine's flesh.' Even the intermediate races see the pallid hue of the European with dislike, and associate it with evil. 'Are the Jews as white as you?' a Dugganah chief asked a fair-complexioned Englishman.—'No, much darker.'—'Really! they are a very bad people. I thought they were quite white.' A gentle-hearted Shoua woman felt impelled to soften by her compassion the misfortune of one of these ill-favored strangers:—'We are so sorry for you that you are white!'

"You must not suppose that the peculiarities of the foreigner are, with the natives, a reason for ill-treating him. It is rare — most rare in Pagan Africa — that the stranger meets with insult or injury, unless he provoke it by his own conduct. If his deportment be reasonably discreet, he is easily recognized as a fellow-being. If he arrive as the king's stranger, that is, having duly announced his visit beforehand to the king or chief, and obtained permission to make it, and if, after his arrival, he pay such conformity to the customs and laws of the country as he would be obliged to do in Europe or the United States, he is sure of hospitality and kindness. In the countries which have become thoroughly Mahometanized, it is probable that regard for the Christian never goes much beyond the humanity and courtesy due to a stranger. But among the Pagan peoples, the guest, if he prove upright and gentlemanly, is soon admitted to esteem, and, should he remain long enough, may even become an object of affection and admiration.

"Here let me interrupt myself to tell you, that, in what I have said of the character of the Africans and their institutions, I have had in view only the black nations of Africa. The inhabitants of the northern and northeastern parts, and those of the extreme south, have not, therefore, been in question. Nor have I meant to include the Moorish and Berber peoples who inhabit or infest the northern part of Negroland. Nothing of all that I have said of the amiable qualities of the black Africans, of the happy condition of their serfs, of the security in which foreigners can travel among them, applies to the Moors and Berbers. The character of the Moors seems to be, in almost every respect, the opposite of that of the negro. Park, who suffered captivity among the Moors, says, 'They are a people who study mischief as a science, and exult in the miseries and misfortunes of their fellow-creatures.' Other travellers give them no better reputation. Let me ask you, when you are reading accounts of Africa, to bear in mind the distinction, and not to make the negro Africans responsible for acts of treachery and violence committed by Moors, or Berbers, or Arabs. Whenever, in this journal, I say 'the Africans,' without more, you will understand that I mean the true sons of Africa, the black men.

" The dislike and apprehension with which the white man is regarded in Africa are, unhappily, but too well founded. These feelings are undoubtedly strengthened, among the Mahometan nations, by religious zeal; but it is not in bigotry that they have had their origin; nor need we look for it in natural antipathy. The Christians very early made for themselves an evil reputation in Africa. When Ca da Mosto entered the Gambia, not a quarter of a century after the Portuguese first surmounted the dangers of Cape Bojador, the natives of the country refused to have anything to do with him. It was in vain that he invited them 'to come peaceably and lovingly and take what goods they chose, giving what they liked in return, or even to take them for nothing.' They answered, that 'they had already some knowledge of the Christians, and had heard of their dealings on the Senegal; that those must be very wicked people who could enter into friendship with them, since it was well understood that they were men-eaters, who bought black people to devour them.' The Portuguese had already at that time, according to Ca da Mosto, established a regular slave-trade; they had a dépôt on the island of Arguim, from which seven or eight hundred slaves were annually shipped for Portugal.

From the time of their first appearance on the African coast, the white men had been the scourge of the country, making continual descents by day and by night, and seizing the inhabitants whom they found at their peaceful occupations or sleeping in supposed security. After the Portuguese, came other of the principal Christian nations in turn, vying with them and with each other in acts of perfidy and cruelty. The fame of these ghastly ogres, first of their fitful atrocities, and afterwards of their more systematic villany, spread through the country; century after century passed, and still the tales of horror that went from the coast inland only multiplied and deepened. Is it to be wondered at that the people of the interior of Africa shrink from these white strangers, whom they have heard of only as chief actors in scenes of violence or baseness? Is it not rather matter of surprise and admiration that they should still be able to judge the Christian with candor, and to lay aside, upon good cause shown, a distrust which it would be unjust to call a prejudice?

"England — whose wrong-doing we must grieve over as our own — has had its own share of guilt towards Africa. But, at least, it has been foremost in the work of atonement.

"It is cheering to find that Englishmen are already making a better reputation for the white man in Africa. The report of their efforts to suppress the slave-trade, and .to establish an honest commerce in its place, has already penetrated the country in many directions. Not only is the Pagan won to them, but even the Mahometan is forced into respect for consistent Christians. 'You are an Englishman; it is enough. Englishmen are of one word.' This assurance of confidence was given to an English traveller by a Tibboo trader. 'You are a beautiful people,' the Felatah Sultan exclaimed, when Clapperton told him that no slave could set foot on English soil.

"The influence of the new system of conduct adopted by the English towards the natives was seen in the reception given to Laing by the Kurankos and Sulimas, which was marked by something more than the benevolence that a well-conducted traveller is almost sure of among the Africans. His fame had gone before him, as the envoy of a powerful and just people, about to propose a reciprocity of kind offices, and the opening of a commerce honorable and profitable on both sides.

"We are now sharing with England in the great work of redemption, which I hope will be carried on with a generous rivalry. But it will be long before we see all the results we wish. Against centuries of depravation, a few years of feeble and imperfect atonement! It becomes us to be patient.

"What a contrast there is between the work which true Christians now propose to themselves in Africa and that which has been carried on there for nearly four hundred years by men bearing the name! When we read of the dealings of the two races with each other, where they have come in contact on African soil, we are forced to feel that the whites are the savages, reckless, cunning, ferocious, and destitute even of the natural sense of honor seldom wholly wanting in the rudest barbarian; while the blacks, in the accounts given of them by their very betrayers and corrupters, are found hospitable, compassionate, courteous; they are found truthful, too, and honest, except so far as they have learned that deception is a part of the whites' system of commerce, and that, with them, knavery and trading are synonymous.

"And men ask how it is that the Africans have profited so little by an intercourse of four centuries with civilized and Christian nations!"

VI.

I HAD to wait for Colvil's plays much longer than I liked. But at last came a fair copy of the first scene of the "Tragedy of Errors." For some time I received an instalment about once a fortnight. Then there was an interval of silence; and then, instead of the continuation of this piece, came some scenes of a Second Part. "I cannot help it," he wrote; "this claimed me, and would not be put off. The First Part is already safe on paper; you are sure of that; but you will never have this, unless you take it now." I saw no good reason why he should not both write the new and transcribe the old. I believe I told him so, and that it was in answer to this reproach that he wrote to me,—

"You forget that I am not a student,—not one of those happy licensed votaries of letters who go into their study in the morning and close the door against the outer world. They can abandon themselves to their visions while the hour lasts, and turn to some piece of duty-work when the imagination is exhausted. Active labor engrosses me from the rising of the sun to its going down. I am not a gentleman farmer, who has men under him better acquainted with his business than he is. I have only hands to aid me; mine must be always the planning, the directing head. Nor does my post of general director exempt me from attention to details. I must be constantly on the alert. Farmers are subject to many surprises and disconcerting accidents. When I have counted confidently on some hours of leisure, a gust of wind or an unseasonable shower has robbed me of them. Our labors are of the most varied kind, and oppose themselves to continuity of thought. When I have the good fortune to be held for some hours together by a monotonous piece of work which leaves my mind untaxed, I seize on this favorable season for reflection or composition. But then I am seldom alone. When my visions begin to throng on me, they are often startled by the very real voice of my good Hans. With a sigh I see them dissolve, never to offer themselves again; for, whatever new combinations my kaleidoscope may present, it never repeats for me precisely the same forms. I cannot put off my faithful German. He does not surmise that I am carrying on an inward work at the same time with the outward one, and thinks to enliven me and himself by a little profitable conversation. I should wound him, if I repelled him. I can lighten his labor by admitting him to a full companionship; I should make it bitter, if I remained wrapped in my own thoughts as if I disdained to share his. Then his sons have a still stronger claim on me: they are young; I am their instructor. The good boys often take occasion, in our common labors, to prove to me, by some remark or apposite question, the accuracy of their memory or the interest they feel in what I have been teaching them. Can I hold back the word of praise which makes happy, or the explanation that furnishes these young minds with new food to work upon, because, in giving it, I must break the thread of my own ideas, or dismiss the spirits who were beginning to obey my call? No, — I must not sacrifice the small, but certain good, to a doubtful one.

"I do not say all this in the way of repining. You know that I count my lot a blessed one. The circumstances in which I am placed, though they frustrate my intention of accomplishment, do not mar my happiness. I enjoy even the hindrances I complain of. As soon as I have overcome the first disappointment, I take real pleasure in my conversations with honest, pedantic Hans. My relation to his boys is a source of great satisfaction to me. Whatever is mine is, I believe, transfigured to me. My poor lands, — when I tried to look at them through your eyes, I saw how flat, how rude, how uninteresting. I know they are not so productive as such an extent of ground ought to be. I have sometimes a misgiving that they were not wisely chosen. Yet there is that about my farm that I would not willingly change it for another.

"If I thought the places in which the lines are fallen to me pleasant before, how doubly pleasant are they now that your idea is associated with them! My room is still your room. You tenant it with me. I turn to you to claim your sympathy when I read, your counsel when I write. I teach you to distinguish the notes of our birds, to call by name the wild-flowers whose successive opening marks the passage of our seasons. My lonely meditations are now animated discussions with you. My mind is quickened by your imagined opposition or approval.

"I live little in the future,—at least, in my own. I have not, like you, in every day a new lifetime. I build no castles in the air: my sphere is inexorably marked out. But the hopes of the world occupy me in default of my own. I long for a better future for its struggling, and still more for its apathetic millions. The destinies of races interest me. And deep in my heart lives and watches a desire to accomplish something while

I am yet on earth. But this latent ambition—if it be ambition—is not of the force to drive me into enterprise. I content myself still with doing each day what belongs to it,—trusting, that, if God has a work for me to perform, He will make it consistent with the dear and sacred duties He has laid on me. These duties hold me here by the couch of my devoted mother.

"All this, dear friend, in answer to your compassion, to your eager desire to see me in a position more congenial to you than this barren, toilsome life of mine would be. But our Author has fitted every being for the place He assigns it. You are born for ease, for success. You have a confident, resolute nature, that would perhaps rebel under suffering, but can deal nobly with prosperity. But do not, therefore, pity a man who would part with his sorrowful recollections even less willingly than with his glad ones, and to whom his privations are possessions."

I will not go over all the trials my patience sustained in waiting on the leisure and the moods of a farmer-poet. I will not enumerate the sowings and reapings, the fellings and pilings, the accidents by flood and drought, that conspired with all the nameless hindrances of a working-man's day to school my impatience and damp my enthusiasm. It sometimes seemed to me that Colvil neglected nothing, postponed nothing, except what I thought most important. I did not abandon my projects, but they ceased to engross me. I resigned myself to let Fate and my friend take their own way, meaning to take mine as soon as possession gave me power. In the mean time I contented myself with Edward's affection and his correspondence, and learned to be almost as well pleased when I received only a proof of his remembrance, in some hasty, hardly legible lines, or a critique of a new book, or a disquisition on some subject we had discussed together, as when I took from the post the well-stuffed envelope which told me, before I opened it, that it held what was to advance me towards my end.

When the Second Part of the "Tragedy of Errors" was at last safe in my hands, I had to submit to another disappointment. Instead of the remaining scenes of the First Part, which I now expected to have as a matter of course, came scenes of a new piece. This was continued until I began to take an interest in its characters, when it was broken off abruptly in favor of a third. I remonstrated. Colvil promised amendment, but begged me to let him go on with the last play he had begun. "I sometimes feel," he said, "a particular attraction towards some piece of work. If I could command all my hours, I would not indulge myself in these caprices. As it is, I find by experience that it is an economy of time. When my fatigue is too great to allow me to set myself task-work, I often find it suspended by an employment to which I am involuntarily drawn." He sent me then the first, second, and fifth acts of the new piece, and some detached scenes from the third and fourth. After this he returned to the copying of the First Part of the "Tragedy of Errors." I received portions at regular intervals without further interruption.

It was on a stormy evening in the month of November that I at last held in my hand the completion of my long baffled desire. I had been passing the day in the country. I returned about seven o'clock, and went immediately to my room and to the little table near my writing-desk, on which were placed the letters and notes that arrived in my absence. I chose from the heap the expected letter: its size and weight answered my question before I broke the seal.

My room was in the back of the house and looked upon the old-fashioned garden. The rain beat threateningly against the windows, through which I could discern a wild tossing of branches and a driving of withered leaves. I felt a thrill of that awe by which man is subdued in the presence of the elements when they put forth their power, even when he knows himself beyond its reach. On my side of the transparent barrier which stood between me and the gloom and tumult was tranquillity and genial glow. The soft flame of a wood-fire, nearly burnt out, flickered on the hearth. The candles were already lighted on the table near which my reading-chair waited for me. The impression which had seemed of foreboding, but was only a touch of sympathy, passed away. I seated myself with a sense of satisfaction which was almost self-gratulation, and gave myself up to the pages of my friend, smiling to think that the rain and fitful wind which were among the adjuncts of his scene would be better represented for me that evening than they were ever likely to be on the stage.

The man who lives much alone — only the more alone, if he have many acquaintances, as I have — finds sympathies and analogies where they are not obvious to another mind: perhaps because his affections and fancy, having no real objects to interest them, occupy themselves with shadows; perhaps because in his solitude he attains to a dim divination of hidden relations, and, unbound by the stronger and closer attachments of human existence, becomes conscious of the less palpable ties. It has often appeared to me, in looking back, that some mysterious relation between the spirit of Colvil and my own gave his imagination an unconscious prophetic power, through which the presentation of scenes and personages that had no resemblance to anything I was conversant with, or that I was probably destined to encounter, stirred in me monitions of chance and change. In the early days of our intercourse, when he first read to me from his dramas, I was more than once visited by these vague intimations. Passages for which I had then no application fixed themselves in my memory by some attraction whose source I did not explore, and came up to me long after as the expression of my own feelings. The coincidence did not the less impress me, that the circumstances which rendered them applicable to me were far other than those with which Colvil had at first combined them.

An association blended of likeness and opposition connected Colvil's "Night" with a night painfully memorable to me. I had so completely lost myself in the imagined scene, that, when, as I turned the last leaf of the manuscript, a sound was heard as of opening and closing doors, and then of quick footsteps approaching my room, the real mingled for an instant with the ideal, and I felt myself in the midst of the agitation and hurried movement of a household among whom death has appeared suddenly. My name, spoken in a tone of pressing alarm, recalled me to myself.

There was no time to be lost, if I would receive the parting blessing of my father.

The death-bed to which I had been summoned bore no resemblance to that at which I had just been present in imagination. My father, a man of irreproachable life, of frank and warm affections, was closing, in the fulness of years, a career whose success had been proportioned to its integrity. He had been, in the strictest sense, a man of business. The conduct of commercial affairs had been not only the occupation, but the pleasure of his life. He had been lynx-eyed for the opportunities of increasing his wealth, and not less prompt in action than keen in discernment. But his millions had rolled up without exciting jealousy, for his hand was as large to dispense as to grasp. He had never forgotten the struggles of his youth. The man who was beginning the hard ascent that he had surmounted looked to him rather with expectation than with envy; for it was known to be his joy, where he discerned a kindred energy, to lighten the obstacles that impeded it. When, after his retirement, he occasionally revisited the scene of his former activity, his white hairs excited a movement of respect, and many an intent man threw aside his preoccupations and pressed forward to clasp the hand which had helped him up the difficult first rounds of Fortune's ladder, or, more beneficent still, had extended rescue, when he had tottered midway in the ascent.

My father's health, which had never before known an hour's failure, broke down suddenly in his sixty-third year. He passed from vigor to old age at one step. He lived five years after this change took place in him, but withdrew from the management of affairs and gradually lost his interest in them. For a year before his death he had only endured existence, and had spoken continually of his release as of something wished and waited for. Yet, as is often the case with long-expected events, the closing hour came upon me at last with all the effect of a surprise. As I stood beside that extended form and looked upon the still features, which, after death, retook the firm and benignant expression of former days, the years of weakness and dependence which had intervened seemed obliterated. An unexpected sense of orphanage fell upon me. It seemed as if a guardianship had been withdrawn which had stood between me and an adverse fate.

My sister was separated from me by a great distance of years, and still more by the seriousness and reserve of her character. The authority which her superiority of age had permitted her to exercise over my childhood, and which, replacing the mild rule of the tenderest of mothers, had seemed to me austere, had established associations with her presence which the more equal intercourse of after-years could not wholly efface. When, therefore, her husband proposed to me that we should continue to occupy together the paternal house, which, by the request of my father, had for several years been their home as well as mine, I declined this arrangement, though I was sensible it was sincerely desired by my brother-in-law, whom I cordially liked.

I removed, then, from my father's house to a hotel, where I established myself, with my little library and my collections of coins and minerals, in apartments whose size and appointments corresponded rather with my fortune than my wishes. They had been selected for me by a friend who had consulted his own tastes more than mine. I would gladly have transferred to him the enjoyment of their magnificence, if the customs of our time had permitted a man to impose an obligation of this kind on his equal. The useless luxuries that charm the imagination of him who cannot command them are often found merely troublesome by one whose wealth gives him the power to have or to reject them. The spaciousness of my rooms seemed to render them only more dreary and unhomelike. The gorgeous modern furniture made the sense of change press more heavily on me, contrasting with the sober, old-fashioned elegance of my father's house.

I was not, however, left solitary. My many friends thronged to offer condolence. I felt that they were far from divining that I might really stand in need of it.

In the midst of the formal friendships and hollow intimacies in which my life was involved, my mind reverted with a sense of rest and reliance to the ties I had formed for myself in a sphere so distant and so different from my own. They seemed to me, connecting as they did my deeper being with the emotions of a simple and earnest heart, more real than any yet existing in which birth or habit had bound me.

While my thoughts were faithful to Colvil, I suffered the many small cares and occupations which necessarily claimed my attention at that period to interrupt my correspondence with him. When I reopened it, it was to find that the time had arrived, which I now know arrives infallibly, when the source of pleasure must be converted into a source of pain.

During the interval between Colvil's last letter and my tardy reply, the part of the country in which his farm lay had been visited by repeated inundations, which had occasioned wide destruction of property and even loss of life.

His own lands suffered; his house was spared, though for a time thought to be in danger. He exerted himself through several successive days and nights in the rescue of his neighbors and their goods. As long as the danger lasted, he was insensible to fatigue and exposure, but was prostrated by fever as soon as the necessity for effort was over. He gave me these particulars in a short letter written in answer to mine. The fever had then left him, and his strength was slowly returning.

A few weeks after, I learned from him that he was once more superintending the labors of his farm. He continued to write to me regularly during the summer. His letters left on my mind a sense of anxiety,—though, studying them closely, I found nothing in their contents which seemed to justify it. My foreboding was answered in the autumn, when I received from him a frank and full communication on the subject of his health. The malady which had proved fatal to his father had declared itself by unmistakable signs. At the same time that he made me this disclosure, Colvil announced his intention of resisting the advances of disease neither by remedies nor by prudence, but by resolution and constant occupation. "I begin this day," he said, "the work on the English language which I have long contemplated, and for which, as you know, I have been collecting materials."

He forwarded to me from time to time, during the autumn and winter, portions of this work. His labors were interrupted in the spring by a new attack of inflammation of the lungs. He surmounted it; but if he had hitherto been under any illusions in regard to his state of health, they were now dispelled. I refused, however, to believe in his danger. I was more disturbed by my apprehensions while they were vague than now that they had a definite object. I recalled many instances of persons attacked by lung complaints at his age, who had, notwithstanding, lived to be old men. I persuaded myself that change of air and scene was all that was needed for his restoration. I urged him to come to me, believing that the comforts and distractions I could offer him would more than counterbalance the greater severity of climate. I ought to have gone to him. But I was detained in New York by some intricate affairs, not my own, which I had undertaken to untangle. It was a responsibility which I had inherited. The business was a delicate one, which could not be confided to a substitute, nor properly postponed. So I felt then. It was one of those barriers between us and action which we suffer ourselves to think impassable while the decisive time is going by, and which we perceive to have been of gossamer when the neglect has become irreparable.

While Edward's health declined, that of his mother seemed strangely to revive. "I cannot help rejoicing in this restoration," he wrote,—"yet why? It will only secure to her the pain of surviving me."

He returned, in these last days, to the subject of our early conversations. He had some time before sketched for me the story of European enterprise in Africa. He now wrote, more fully than he had yet done, of the Africans themselves,—collecting from early and late authorities evidence of their claims to respect, and showing what testimony had been borne, even by unfriendly witnesses, to their courage, their intelligence, their industry, and their humanity. From the Africans of Africa he passed to those of the United States, and gave me his views of their characteristics and deserts. "I have continued to write to you on this subject," he said in conclusion, "because I have seen that your interest in it is real, and you are in a position to render service in one way or another to these our disinherited brothers, who cannot plead with us for themselves unless through their trust and helplessness."

My hopes were confirmed. But I soon found that Colvil's cheerfulness had another source than

I had supposed. He was not looking forward to prolonged life; he had reconciled himself with death. He was ready to surrender himself into the hands of his Maker, and enter whatever sphere His wisdom judged fittest.

This was revealed to me in a letter full of tenderness, which I received in October, 184—. About a fortnight after came one from his mother, bringing me his farewell and hers.

Mrs. Colvil desired me to consider the manuscripts in my possession, and those which were to be forwarded to me after her death, as my own, and to do with them what my judgment and my affection for the writer should dictate. She recommended to my protection the poor lonely Tabitha, who, by her advice, was about to find her new home in a Free State. A few lines, added by another hand, told me that the mother and son were already reunited.

The grief of this bereavement was mitigated to me by the new ties I soon after formed.

My wife, beautiful and high-spirited, lived even more in the actual world than I did. The legacy of the obscure poet could have no importance for her. I shrank from the pain of an unanswered claim on her sympathy. Perhaps I hesitated to submit the objects of a superstitious affection to her impartial judgment. Colvil's manuscripts remained, not forgotten, but untouched, in the drawers where I had first placed them, until I committed them, with other valuable papers, to the charge of a friend, on my departure for Europe, a few years after my marriage, with my wife and our two children.

Our time in Europe passed pleasantly and rapidly. I was recalled by the sudden death of the real head of the commercial house that had been founded by my father, and of which I was nominally the senior partner. This man had entered my father's service in a humble capacity, but, showing superior abilities, soon obtained employment better suited to them. He became a clerk in the house in which he had been errand-boy, and was gradually advanced by his own talents and my father's appreciation of them, until he became the partner of his patron. My father in his latter years abandoned to him entirely the conduct of the business. I gladly left it in his hands when I succeeded to the paternal place and fortune.

But I was now called upon to look into my affairs, and either to assume their management myself, or find some person in whom I could repose the same confidence I had placed in the tried pupil and associate of my father. I felt this summons to immerse myself in business as an unpleasant interruption of my life of leisure, but I was far from foreboding the changes of which it was the precursor.

I had lived in New York from my childhood, but the memory of an earlier home had always been cherished in my father's house. My wife was of New York both by birth and predilection. Not even Paris could supersede it in her regard. She easily consoled herself for the curtailment of our European plans, and looked forward gayly to finding herself among old scenes and old acquaintances. She enjoyed, too, the prospect of entering once more the domain of which she had been queen, and of reassuming the cares and dignities of domestic government. As we approached the shore, her pleasure in the return was so lively, she was so animated in recounting her various projects and in picturing the comforts of our future life, that I found my own thoughts gradually drawn into the same channel, and my last regrets for Europe faded as I imagined myself again seated by my own fireside, among my own pictures and my own books, and taking up once more all the old familiar habits.

My brother-in-law came down to the steamer to meet us. My first glance at his face told me he was not there merely to welcome me.

"What is it? What have I to learn?" He had come to announce to me his own ruin and mine.

The insolvency of the commercial house in which

my sister's fortune as well as my own was invested had been whispered at the death-bed of its active head; it had been proclaimed as soon as the funeral solemnities were over. The credit of the house was deeply buried under the mass of claims before I arrived to take my part in the labors and humiliations which devolved on the surviving partners. Its embarrassments were of long date. They had their origin in the daring schemes of the adventurous spirit that had had the control of its affairs. Beginning the world with no capital but his own energy and craft, he had steadily advanced in prosperity up to the time when he was left to wield alone the immense resources of the firm in which he had been a subordinate. He was then at the pinnacle of success. But his was not a mind to repose upon victory. It was not cupidity that actuated him, nor a desire for the splendors and indulgences of wealth:—he lived frugally; his family retained the habits of earlier years:—it was pure ambition, the love of conquest. When he found the battle turning against him, he did not despair of his fortune or his strength. He maintained for years a hand-to-hand contest with ruin, disputing every inch of ground, and laying down his arms at last only at the edge of the grave. Peace to his memory! He sleeps with Napoleon and the other baffled ambitious.

The first time I entered what had been my own door, it was in company with the auctioneer who was to preside over the desecration of my household gods.

I did not bear my reverses with equanimity. I maintained an outward composure, but I suffered keenly. The changed prospects of my children tortured me to that degree that their presence was almost a pain to me. It seemed as if my very love for them was obscured by my care for their interests.

My wife retained her cheerfulness through all. One would have thought she had been all her life practising the art of making a little go its farthest. She appeared to enjoy her triumphs in this line, and made light of privation and fatigue. But her courage failed to cheer me. I questioned the reality of her fortitude, conscious of the unsoundness of my own. Wealth, which I thought I hardly valued while I had it, appeared now the supreme good. Life had but one thing to offer me: the restoration of my fortune. During the months of forced inactivity which followed my change of condition, my impatience was exasperated by the consciousness that my reputation as an indolent man of leisure must act as an obstacle to my desires.

Let me not be misunderstood. I have nothing

to say of summer friends, or of "hard unkindness' altered eye." Those who had been kind before were kinder now. Marks of sympathy and offers of service came to us from persons who had never made any profession of regard in the season of our prosperity. Men whom I had formerly benefited, and who had never before spoken of a sense of obligation, came forward to express their gratitude, and to ask me to point out a way for them to prove it. To all these proposals I had one answer:— "Open me a way to work."

The opening was found. A post was offered me in a distant part of the world. The climate was unhealthy, but the compensation was in proportion to the risk. Besides, the position was one which might offer great opportunities to a man who knew how to avail himself of them. I did not hesitate.

My wife wished to go with me. I did not consent. The climate would have been fatal to the young constitution of our children,—now three in number,—and I could not take their mother from them.

Circumstances favored me. I had the courage and the clear sight of a destitute man. At the end of three years I might have gone home satisfied. My wife urged my return. But now I would secure to my family, not only ease, but the old profusion. So keen was my interest in my work that I was hardly conscious of the lapse of time.

I was recalled to a sense of it by news of the death of my wife, who had sunk, worn out by anxiety and hope deferred. This event, for which her letters, always cheerful, though sometimes tenderly reproachful, had not prepared me, waked me to a keen remorse. I quieted it by resolving to make the only atonement in my power, by devoting myself more than ever to the interests of her children. I gave myself with greater ardor than before to the reconstruction of my fortune. Death struck again and again before I came to the consciousness, that, while I was gathering gold, the real treasures of my life were passing from me unenjoyed. The flood of parental tenderness, so long diked off, suddenly burst through and inundated my whole being. I could not make my arrangements for the return fast enough.

It is not my own history that I am here to relate. I need not, then, tell of the happiness of restoration to my only child, — of the anxiety that broke in upon it, — of the voyage to Cuba, — of the grave I left there. It is enough to say that I am now alone with my wealth.

Having no interests in the present or the future, I live in the past: not the near past; its regrets are still too bitter.

I find a frequent solace in retracing the episode of my acquaintance with Colvil. I have taken from the trunk, where I put them on my departure for Europe, the manuscripts confided to me in their freshness with so many hopes and doubts, but now dim and discolored by time, and having interest for no human eye but mine.

I have read them over: not critically, — I am even less a judge of literary works than in my youth, — but taking all for granted, and giving myself up to them. I feel that I could again answer the question I saw in Colvil's eye, when he had concluded his first evening's reading, as I did then: Yes, it interests me. It even seems that now deeper chords in my being are touched, and that I comprehend better the scope of the writer than when I sat by his side and listened to his voice. Perhaps my sympathies, quickened and enlarged by suffering, are now more capable of following his. I feel, as I did not then, the force of the motto he had written in pencil on one of the blank leaves of the "Tragedy of Errors:" —

"Aux plus déshérités le plus d'amour."

I called to mind the hopes of which I had been the confidant, and asked myself whether the trembling prayer of the mother, that her son's life on this earth should not be wholly in vain, might not be answered through me. I have ventured to make the trial.

I know it is very possible I am under the influence of an illusion. Perhaps, having so familiarized myself with Colvil's creations that they have almost become a part of my life, as they once were of his, I have lost the power of distinguishing between their real interest and that which my affection and my isolation have lent them. If this be so, — if, in doing what I regard as an act of duty, I am in fact committing an indiscretion,—if the gift which I offer in the name of my friend be not found worthy of acceptance, — the mistake is not his. Let it count as one more among the errors of my life. It will remain to me but to avow it, and to ask pardon of the public and of him.

☞ Any Books in this list will be sent free of postage, on receipt of price.

BOSTON, 135 WASHINGTON STREET,
OCTOBER, 1861.

A LIST OF BOOKS

PUBLISHED BY

TICKNOR AND FIELDS.

Sir Walter Scott.

ILLUSTRATED HOUSEHOLD EDITION OF THE WAVERLEY NOVELS. 50 volumes. In portable size, 16mo. form. Now Complete. Price 75 cents a volume.

The paper is of fine quality; the stereotype plates are not old ones repaired, the type having been cast expressly for this edition. The Novels are illustrated with capital steel plates engraved in the best manner, after drawings and paintings by the most eminent artists, among whom are Birket Foster, Darley, Billings, Landseer, Harvey, and Faed. This Edition contains all the latest notes and corrections of the author, a Glossary and Index; and some curious additions, especially in "Guy Mannering" and the "Bride of Lammermoor;" being the fullest edition of the Novels ever published. *The notes are at the foot of the page*,—a great convenience to the reader.

Any of the following Novels sold separate.

WAVERLEY, 2 vols.
GUY MANNERING, 2 vols.
THE ANTIQUARY, 2 vols.
ROB ROY, 2 vols.
OLD MORTALITY, 2 vols.
BLACK DWARF, } 2 vols.
LEGEND OF MONTROSE, }
HEART OF MID LOTHIAN, 2 vols.
BRIDE OF LAMMERMOOR, 2 vols.
IVANHOE, 2 vols.
THE MONASTERY, 2 vols.
THE ABBOT, 2 vols.
KENILWORTH, 2 vols.
THE PIRATE, 2 vols.
THE FORTUNES OF NIGEL, 2 vols.
PEVERIL OF THE PEAK, 2 vols.
QUENTIN DURWARD, 2 vols.
ST. RONAN'S WELL, 2 vols.
REDGAUNTLET, 2 vols.
THE BETROTHED, } 2 vols.
THE HIGHLAND WIDOW, }
THE TALISMAN, }
TWO DROVERS, }
MY AUNT MARGARET'S MIRROR, } 2 vols.
THE TAPESTRIED CHAMBER, }
THE LAIRD'S JOCK, }
WOODSTOCK, 2 vols.
THE FAIR MAID OF PERTH, 2 vols.
ANNE OF GEIERSTEIN, 2 vols.
COUNT ROBERT OF PARIS, 2 vols.
THE SURGEON'S DAUGHTER, }
CASTLE DANGEROUS, } 2 vols.
INDEX AND GLOSSARY, }

TALES OF A GRANDFATHER. *In Press.*

LIFE. By J. G. Lockhart. *In Press.* Uniform with Novels. Vols. 1 and 2 now ready. Cloth. $1.50.

Thomas De Quincey.

CONFESSIONS OF AN ENGLISH OPIUM-EATER, AND SUSPIRIA DE PROFUNDIS. With Portrait. 75 cents.

BIOGRAPHICAL ESSAYS. 75 cents.

MISCELLANEOUS ESSAYS. 75 cents.

THE CÆSARS. 75 cents.

LITERARY REMINISCENCES. 2 vols. $1.50.

NARRATIVE AND MISCELLANEOUS PAPERS. 2 vols. $1.50.

ESSAYS ON THE POETS, &c. 1 vol. 16mo. 75 cents.

HISTORICAL AND CRITICAL ESSAYS. 2 vols. $1.50.

AUTOBIOGRAPHIC SKETCHES. 1 vol. 75 cents.

ESSAYS ON PHILOSOPHICAL WRITERS, &c. 2 vols. 16mo. $1.50.

LETTERS TO A YOUNG MAN, AND OTHER PAPERS. 1 vol. 75 cents.

THEOLOGICAL ESSAYS AND OTHER PAPERS. 2 vols. $1.50.

THE NOTE BOOK. 1 vol. 75 cents.

MEMORIALS AND OTHER PAPERS. 2 vols. 16mo. $1.50.

THE AVENGER AND OTHER PAPERS. 1 vol. 75 cents.

LOGIC OF POLITICAL ECONOMY, AND OTHER PAPERS. 1 vol. 75 cents.

Thomas Hood.

MEMORIALS. Edited by his Children. 2 vols. $1.75.

Alfred Tennyson.

POETICAL WORKS. With Portrait. 2 vols. Cloth. $2.00.

POCKET EDITION OF POEMS COMPLETE. 2 vols. $1.50.

POEMS. Complete in one volume. With Portrait. $1.00.

THE PRINCESS. Cloth. 50 cents.

IN MEMORIAM. Cloth. 75 cents.

MAUD, AND OTHER POEMS. Cloth. 50 cents.

IDYLLS OF THE KING. A new volume. Cloth. 75 cents.

Charles Dickens.

[ENGLISH EDITION.]

THE COMPLETE WORKS OF CHARLES DICKENS. Fine Library Edition. Published simultaneously in London and Boston. English print, fine cloth binding, 22 vols. 12mo. $27.50.

Henry W. Longfellow.

POETICAL WORKS. 2 vols. Boards, $2.00. Cloth, $2.25.

POCKET EDITION OF POETICAL WORKS. In two volumes. $1.75.

POCKET EDITION OF PROSE WORKS COMPLETE. In two volumes. $1.75.

THE SONG OF HIAWATHA. $1.00.

EVANGELINE: A Tale of Acadia. 75 cents.

THE GOLDEN LEGEND. A Poem. $1.00.

HYPERION. A Romance. $1.00.

OUTRE-MER. A Pilgrimage. $1.00.

KAVANAGH. A Tale. 75 cents.

THE COURTSHIP OF MILES STANDISH. 1 vol. 16mo. 75 cents.

Illustrated editions of EVANGELINE. POEMS, HYPERION, THE GOLDEN LEGEND, and MILES STANDISH.

Charles Reade.

PEG WOFFINGTON. A Novel. 75 cents.

CHRISTIE JOHNSTONE. A Novel. 75 cents.

CLOUDS AND SUNSHINE. A Novel. 75 cents.

"NEVER TOO LATE TO MEND." 2 vols. $1.50.

WHITE LIES. A Novel. 1 vol. $1.25.

PROPRIA QUÆ MARIBUS and THE BOX TUNNEL. 25 cts.

THE EIGHTH COMMANDMENT. 75 cents.

James Russell Lowell.

Complete Poetical Works. In Blue and Gold. 2 vols. $1.50.
Poetical Works. 2 vols. 16mo. Cloth. $1.50.
Sir Launfal. New Edition. 25 cents.
A Fable for Critics. New Edition. 50 cents.
The Biglow Papers. New Edition. 63 cents.
Fireside Travels. *In Press.*

Nathaniel Hawthorne.

Twice-Told Tales. Two volumes. $1.50.
The Scarlet Letter. 75 cents.
The House of the Seven Gables. $1.00.
The Snow Image, and other Tales. 75 cents.
The Blithedale Romance. 75 cents.
Mosses from an Old Manse. 2 vols. $1.50.
The Marble Faun. 2 vols. $1.50.
True Stories. 75 cents.
A Wonder-Book for Girls and Boys. 75 cents.
Tanglewood Tales. 88 cents.

Edwin P. Whipple.

Essays and Reviews. 2 vols. $2.00.
Lectures on Literature and Life. 63 cents.
Washington and the Revolution. 20 cents.

Charles Kingsley.

Two Years Ago. A New Novel. $1.25.
Amyas Leigh. A Novel. $1.25.
Glaucus; or, the Wonders of the Shore. 50 cts.
Poetical Works. 75 cents.
The Heroes; or, Greek Fairy Tales. 75 cents.
Andromeda and other Poems. 50 cents.
Sir Walter Raleigh and his Time, &c. $1.25.
New Miscellanies. 1 vol. $1.00.

Mrs. Howe.

Passion Flowers. 75 cents.

Words for the Hour. 75 cents.

The World's Own. 50 cents.

A Trip to Cuba. 1 vol. 16mo. 75 cents.

George S. Hillard.

Six Months in Italy. 1 vol. 16mo. $1.50.

Dangers and Duties of the Mercantile Profession. 25 cents.

Selections from the Writings of Walter Savage Landor. 1 vol. 16mo. 75 cents.

Oliver Wendell Holmes.

Elsie Venner : a Romance of Destiny. 2 vols. Cloth. $1.75.

Poems. With fine Portrait. Cloth. $1.00.

Astræa. Fancy paper. 25 cents.

The Autocrat of the Breakfast Table. With Illustrations by Hoppin. 16mo. $1.00.

The Same. Large Paper Edition. 8vo. Tinted paper. $3.00.

The Professor at the Breakfast Table. 16mo. $1.00.

The Same. Large Paper Edition. 8vo. Tinted paper. $3.00.

Songs in Many Keys. A new volume. *In Press.*

Currents and Counter-Currents, and other Medical Essays. 1 vol. Cloth. $1.25.

Ralph Waldo Emerson.

Essays. 1st Series. 1 vol. $1.00.

Essays. 2d Series. 1 vol. $1.00.

Miscellanies. 1 vol. $1.00.

Representative Men. 1 vol. $1.00.

English Traits. 1 vol. $1.00.

Poems. 1 vol. $1.00.

Conduct of Life. 1 vol. $1.00.

Goethe.

WILHELM MEISTER. Translated by *Carlyle.* 2 vols. $2.50.

FAUST. Translated by *Hayward.* 75 cents.

FAUST. Translated by *Charles T. Brooks.* $1.00.

CORRESPONDENCE WITH A CHILD. *Bettina.* 1 vol. 12mo. $1.25.

Henry Giles.

LECTURES, ESSAYS, &c. 2 vols. $1.50.

DISCOURSES ON LIFE. 75 cents.

ILLUSTRATIONS OF GENIUS. Cloth. $1.00.

John G. Whittier.

POCKET EDITION OF POETICAL WORKS. 2 vols. $1.50.

OLD PORTRAITS AND MODERN SKETCHES. 75 cents.

MARGARET SMITH'S JOURNAL. 75 cents.

SONGS OF LABOR, AND OTHER POEMS. Boards. 50 cts.

THE CHAPEL OF THE HERMITS. Cloth. 50 cents.

LITERARY RECREATIONS, &c. Cloth. $1.00.

THE PANORAMA, AND OTHER POEMS. Cloth. 50 cents.

HOME BALLADS AND POEMS. A new volume. 75 cents.

Capt. Mayne Reid.

THE PLANT HUNTERS. With Plates. 75 cents.

THE DESERT HOME: OR, THE ADVENTURES OF A LOST FAMILY IN THE WILDERNESS. With fine Plates. $1.00.

THE BOY HUNTERS. With fine Plates. 75 cents.

THE YOUNG VOYAGEURS: OR, THE BOY HUNTERS IN THE NORTH. With Plates. 75 cents.

THE FOREST EXILES. With fine Plates. 75 cents.

THE BUSH BOYS. With fine Plates. 75 cents.

THE YOUNG YAGERS. With fine Plates. 75 cents.

RAN AWAY TO SEA: AN AUTOBIOGRAPHY FOR BOYS. With fine Plates. 75 cents.

THE BOY TAR: A VOYAGE IN THE DARK. A New Book. With fine Plates. 75 cents.

ODD PEOPLE. With Plates. 75 cents.

The Same. Cheap Edition. With Plates. 50 cents.

BRUIN: OR, THE GRAND BEAR HUNT. With Plates. 75 cts.

Rev. F. W. Robertson.

SERMONS. First Series, $1.00.
" Second " $1.00.
" Third " $1.00.
" Fourth " $1.00.

LECTURES AND ADDRESSES ON LITERARY AND SOCIAL TOPICS. $1.00.

Mrs. Jameson.

CHARACTERISTICS OF WOMEN. Blue and Gold. 75 cents.
LOVES OF THE POETS. " " 75 cents.
DIARY OF AN ENNUYÉE. " " 75 cents.
SKETCHES OF ART, &c. " " 75 cents.
STUDIES AND STORIES. " " 75 cents.
ITALIAN PAINTERS. " " 75 cents.
LEGENDS OF THE MADONNA. " " 75 cents.
SISTERS OF CHARITY. 1 vol. 16mo. 75 cents.

Grace Greenwood.

GREENWOOD LEAVES. 1st and 2d Series. $1.25 each.

POETICAL WORKS. With fine Portrait. 75 cents.

HISTORY OF MY PETS. With six fine Engravings. Scarlet cloth. 50 cents.

RECOLLECTIONS OF MY CHILDHOOD. With six fine Engravings. Scarlet cloth. 50 cents.

HAPS AND MISHAPS OF A TOUR IN EUROPE. $1.25.

MERRIE ENGLAND. 75 cents.

A FOREST TRAGEDY, AND OTHER TALES. $1.00.

STORIES AND LEGENDS. 75 cents.

STORIES FROM FAMOUS BALLADS. Illustrated. 50 cents.

BONNIE SCOTLAND. Illustrated. 75 cents.

Mrs. Mowatt.

AUTOBIOGRAPHY OF AN ACTRESS. $1.25.

PLAYS. ARMAND AND FASHION. 50 cents.

MIMIC LIFE. 1 vol. $1.25.

THE TWIN ROSES. 1 vol. 75 cents.

Samuel Smiles.

LIFE OF GEORGE STEPHENSON, ENGINEER. $1.00.

SELF HELP; WITH ILLUSTRATIONS OF CHARACTER AND CONDUCT. With Portrait. 1 vol. 75 cents.

BRIEF BIOGRAPHIES. With Plates. $1.25.

Miss Cummins.

EL FUREIDIS. By the Author of "The Lamplighter," &c. $1.00.

Thomas Hughes.

SCHOOL DAYS AT RUGBY. By *An Old Boy.* 1 vol. 16mo. $1.00.

The Same. Illustrated edition. $1.50.

THE SCOURING OF THE WHITE HORSE, OR THE LONG VACATION HOLIDAY OF A LONDON CLERK. By *The Author of "School Days at Rugby."* 1 vol. 16mo. $1.00.

TOM BROWN AT OXFORD. A Sequel to School Days at Rugby. 2 vols. 16mo. With fine Steel Portrait of the Author. $2.00.

François Arago.

BIOGRAPHIES OF DISTINGUISHED SCIENTIFIC MEN. 16mo. 2 vols. $2.00.

Bayard Taylor.

POEMS OF HOME AND TRAVEL. Cloth. 75 cents.

POEMS OF THE ORIENT. Cloth. 75 cents.

A POET'S JOURNAL. *In Press.*

John Neal.

TRUE WOMANHOOD. A Novel. 1 vol. $1.25.

Hans Christian Andersen.

THE SAND-HILLS OF JUTLAND. 1 vol. 16mo. 75 cents.

R. H. Dana, Jr.

To Cuba and Back, a Vacation Voyage, by the Author of "Two Years before the Mast." 75 cents.

Miscellaneous Works in Poetry and Prose.

[poetry.]

Alford's (Henry) Poems. 1 vol. 16mo. Cloth. $1.00.
Angel in the House: The Betrothal. 1 vol. 16mo. Cloth. 75 cents.
" " The Espousals. 1 vol. 16mo. Cloth. 75 cents.
Arnold's (Matthew) Poems. 1 vol. 75 cents.
Aytoun's Bothwell. A Narrative Poem. 1 vol. 75 cents.
Bailey's (P. J.) The Mystic. 1 vol. 16mo. Cloth. 50 cents.
" " The Age. 1 vol. 16mo. Cloth. 75 cents.
Barry Cornwall's English Songs and other Poems. 1 vol. $1.00.
" " Dramatic Poems. 1 vol. $1.00.
Boker's Plays and Poems. 2 vols. 16mo. Cloth. $2.00.
Brooks' German Lyrics. 1 vol. $1.00.
" Faust. A new Translation. 1 vol. $1.00.
Browning's (Robert) Poems. 2 vols. $2.00.
" " Men and Women. 1 vol. $1.00.
Cary's (Alice) Poems. 1 vol. $1.00.
Cary's (Phœbe) Poems and Parodies. 1 vol. 75 cts.
Fresh Hearts that Failed. By the Author of "The New Priest." 1 vol. 50 cents.
Hayne's Poems. 1 vol. 63 cents.
" Avolio and other Poems. 1 vol. 16mo. Cloth. 75 cents.
Hunt's (Leigh) Poems. 2 vols. Blue and Gold. $1.50.
" " Rimini. 1 vol. 50 cents.
Hymns of the Ages. 1 vol. Enlarged edition. $1.25.
Hymns of the Ages. 2d Series. 1 vol. $1.25.
The Same. 8vo. Bevelled boards. Each volume, $3.00.
Johnson's (Rosa V.) Poems. 1 vol. $1.00.
Kemble's (Mrs.) Poems. 1 vol. $1.00.

LOCKHART'S (J. G.) SPANISH BALLADS. With Portrait. 1 vol. 75 cents.

LUNT'S (GEO.) LYRIC POEMS. 1 vol. 16mo. Cloth. 63 cents.

" " JULIA. 1 vol. 50 cents.

MACKAY'S POEMS. 1 vol. $1.00.

MASSEY'S (GERALD) POEMS. 1 vol. Blue and Gold. 75 cents.

MEMORY AND HOPE. A Collection of Consolatory Pieces. 1 vol. $2.00.

MILNES'S POEMS. 1 vol. 88 cents.

MOTHERWELL'S POEMS. 1 vol. Blue and Gold. 75 cts.

" MINSTRELSY, ANCIENT AND MODERN. 2 vols. $1.50.

MULOCH'S (MISS) POEMS. (By Author of "John Halifax.") 1 vol. 75 cents.

OWEN MEREDITH'S POEMS. 1 vol. Blue and Gold. 75 cents.

PARSONS'S POEMS. 1 vol. $1.00.

" DANTE'S INFERNO. Translated. *In Press.*

PERCIVAL'S POEMS. 2 vols. Blue and Gold. $1.75.

QUINCY'S (J. P.) CHARICLES. A Dramatic Poem. 1 vol. 50 cents.

" " LYTERIA: A Dramatic Poem. 50 cents.

READ'S (T. BUCHANAN) POEMS. New and complete edition. 2 vols. $2.00.

REJECTED ADDRESSES. By Horace and James Smith. New edition. 1 vol. 63 cents.

SARGENT'S (EPES) POEMS. 1 vol. 50 cents.

SAXE'S (J. G.) POEMS. With Portrait. 1 vol. 75 cents.

" " THE MONEY KING AND OTHER POEMS. With new Portrait. 1 vol. 75 cents.

SMITH'S (ALEXANDER) LIFE DRAMA. 1 vol. 50 cents.

" " CITY POEMS. 1 vol. 63 cents.

" " EDWIN OF DEIRA. With Portrait. 75 cent.

STODDARD'S (R. H.) POEMS. 1 vol. 63 cents.

" " SONGS OF SUMMER. 1 vol. 75 cts.

SPRAGUE'S (CHARLES) POETICAL AND PROSE WORKS. With Portrait. 1 vol. 88 cents.

THACKERAY'S BALLADS. 1 vol. 75 cents.

THALATTA. A Book for the Seaside. 1 vol. 75 cents.

TUCKERMAN'S POEMS. 1 vol. 75 cents.

WARRENIANA. 1 vol. 63 cents.

[PROSE.]

ALLSTON'S MONALDI. A Tale. 1 vol. 16mo. Cloth. 75 cents.

DANA'S (R. H.) TO CUBA AND BACK. 1 vol. 16mo. Cloth. 75 cents.

DUFFERIN'S (LORD) YACHT VOYAGE. 1 vol. 16mo. Cloth. $1.00.

EL FUREIDIS. By the author of "The Lamplighter." 1 vol. 16mo. Cloth. $1.00.

ERNEST CARROLL; OR, ARTIST-LIFE IN ITALY. 1 vol. 16mo. Cloth. 88 cents.

FREMONT'S LIFE, EXPLORATIONS, AND PUBLIC SERVICES. By C. W. Upham. With Illustrations. 1 vol. 16mo. Cloth. 75 cents.

GASKELL'S (MRS.) RUTH. A Novel. 8vo. Paper. 38 cts.

GUESSES AT TRUTH. By Two Brothers. 1 vol. 12mo. $1.50.

GREENWOOD'S (F. W. P.) SERMONS OF CONSOLATION. 16mo. Cloth, $1.00; cloth, gilt edge, $1.50; morocco, plain gilt edge, $2.00; morocco, extra gilt edge, $2.50.

" HISTORY OF THE KING'S CHAPEL, BOSTON. 12mo. Cloth. 50 cents.

HODSON'S SOLDIER'S LIFE IN INDIA. 1 vol. 16mo. Cloth. $1.00.

HOWITT'S (WILLIAM) LAND, LABOR, AND GOLD. 2 vols. $2.00.

" " A BOY'S ADVENTURES IN AUSTRALIA. 75 cents.

HOWITT'S (ANNA MARY) AN ART STUDENT IN MUNICH. $1.25.

" " A SCHOOL OF LIFE. A Story. 75 cents.

HUFELAND'S ART OF PROLONGING LIFE. 1 vol. 16mo. Cloth. 75 cents.

JERROLD'S (DOUGLAS) LIFE. By his Son. 1 vol. 16mo. Cloth. $1.00.

" " WIT. By his Son. 1 vol. 16mo. Cloth. 75 cents.

JUDSON'S (MRS. E. C.) ALDERBROOK. By Fanny Forrester. 2 vols. $1.75.

" " THE KATHAYAN SLAVE, AND OTHER PAPERS. 1 vol. 63 cents.

" " MY TWO SISTERS: A SKETCH FROM MEMORY. 50 cents.

KAVANAGH'S (JULIA) SEVEN YEARS. 8vo. Paper. 30 cents.

KINGSLEY'S (HENRY) GEOFFRY HAMLYN. 1 vol. 12mo. Cloth. $1.25.

KRAPF'S TRAVELS AND RESEARCHES IN EASTERN AFRICA. 1 vol. 12mo. Cloth. $1.25.

LESLIE'S (C. R.) AUTOBIOGRAPHICAL RECOLLECTIONS. Edited by Tom Taylor. With Portrait. 1 vol. 12mo. Cloth. $1.25.

LAKE HOUSE. From the German of Fanny Lewald. 1 vol. 16mo. Cloth. 75 cents.

LOWELL'S (REV. DR. CHARLES) PRACTICAL SERMONS. 1 vol. 12mo. Cloth. $1.25.

" " OCCASIONAL SERMONS. With fine Portrait. 1 vol. 12mo. Cloth. $1.25.

LIGHT ON THE DARK RIVER; OR, MEMOIRS OF MRS. HAMLIN. 1 vol. 16mo. Cloth. $1.00.

The Same. 16mo. Cloth, gilt edge. $1.50.

LONGFELLOW (REV. S.) AND JOHNSON (REV. S.) A book of Hymns for Public and Private Devotion. 6th edition. 63 cents.

LABOR AND LOVE. A Tale of English Life. 1 vol. 16mo. Cloth. 50 cents.

LEE'S (MRS. E. B.) MEMOIR OF THE BUCKMINSTERS. $1.25.

" " FLORENCE, THE PARISH ORPHAN. 50 cents.

" " PARTHENIA. 1 vol. 16mo. $1.00.

LUNT'S (GEORGE) THREE ERAS IN THE HISTORY OF NEW ENGLAND. 1 vol. $1.00.

MADEMOISELLE MORI: A Tale of Modern Rome. 1 vol. 12mo. Cloth. $1.25.

M'CLINTOCK'S NARRATIVE OF THE SEARCH FOR SIR JOHN FRANKLIN. Library edition. With Maps and Illustrations. 1 vol. small 8vo. $1.50.

The Same. Popular Edition. 1 vol. 12mo. 75 cents.

MANN'S (HORACE) THOUGHTS FOR A YOUNG MAN. 1 vol. 25 cents.

" " SERMONS. 1 vol. $1.00.

MANN'S (MRS. HORACE) PHYSIOLOGICAL COOKERY-BOOK. 1 vol. 16mo. Cloth. 63 cents.

MELVILLE'S HOLMBY HOUSE. A Novel. 8vo. Paper. 50 cents.

MITFORD'S (MISS) OUR VILLAGE. Illustrated. 2 vols. 16mo. $2.50.

" " ATHERTON, AND OTHER STORIES. 1 vol. 16mo. $1.25.

MORLEY'S LIFE OF PALISSY THE POTTER. 2 vols. 16mo. Cloth. $1.50.

MOUNTFORD'S THORPE. 1 vol. 16mo. Cloth. $1.00.

NORTON'S (C. E.) TRAVEL AND STUDY IN ITALY. 1 vol. 16mo. Cloth. 75 cents.

NEW TESTAMENT. A very handsome edition, fine paper and clear type. 12mo. Sheep binding, plain, $1.00; roan, plain, $1.50; calf, plain, $1.75; calf, gilt edge, $2.00; Turkey morocco, plain, $2.50; do. gilt edge, $3.00.

OTIS'S (MRS. H. G.) THE BARCLAYS OF BOSTON. 1 vol. Cloth. $1.25.

PARSONS'S (THEOPHILUS) LIFE. By his Son. 1 vol. 12mo. Cloth. $1.50.

PRESCOTT'S HISTORY OF THE ELECTRIC TELEGRAPH. Illustrated. 1 vol. 12mo. Cloth. $1.75.

POORE'S (BEN PERLEY) LOUIS PHILIPPE. 1 vol. 12mo. Cloth. $1.00.

PHILLIPS'S ELEMENTARY TREATISE ON MINERALOGY. With numerous additions to the Introduction. By Francis Alger. With numerous Engravings. 1 vol. New edition in press.

PRIOR'S LIFE OF EDMUND BURKE. 2 vols. 16mo. Cloth. $2.00.

RAB AND HIS FRIENDS. By John Brown, M. D. Illustrated. 15 cents.

SALA'S JOURNEY DUE NORTH. 1 vol. 16mo. Cloth. $1.00.

SCOTT'S (SIR WALTER) IVANHOE. In one handsome volume. $1.75.

SIDNEY'S (SIR PHILIP) LIFE. By Mrs. Davis. 1 vol. Cloth. $1.00.

SHELLEY MEMORIALS. Edited by the Daughter-in-law of the Poet. 1 vol. 16mo. 75 cents.

SWORD AND GOWN. By the Author of "Guy Livingstone." 1 vol. 16mo. Cloth. 75 cents.

SHAKSPEAR'S (CAPTAIN H.) WILD SPORTS OF INDIA. 1 vol. 16mo. Cloth. 75 cents.

SEMI-DETACHED HOUSE. A Novel. 1 vol. 16mo. Cloth. 75 cents.

SMITH'S (WILLIAM) THORNDALE; OR, THE CONFLICT OF OPINIONS. 1 vol. 12mo. Cloth. $1.25.

SUMNER'S (CHARLES) ORATIONS AND SPEECHES. 2 vols. 16mo. Cloth. $2.50.

ST. JOHN'S (BAYLE) VILLAGE LIFE IN EGYPT. 2 vols. 16mo. Cloth. $1.25.

TYNDALL'S (PROFESSOR) GLACIERS OF THE ALPS. With Illustrations. 1 vol. Cloth. $1.50.

TYLL OWLGLASS'S ADVENTURES. With Illustrations by Crowquill. 1 vol. Cloth, gilt. $2.50.

THE SOLITARY OF JUAN FERNANDEZ. By the Author of "Picciola." 1 vol. 16mo. Cloth. 50 cents.

TAYLOR'S (HENRY) NOTES FROM LIFE. 1 vol. 16mo. Cloth. 50 cents.

TRELAWNY'S RECOLLECTIONS OF SHELLEY AND BYRON. 1 vol. 16mo. Cloth. 75 cents.

THOREAU'S WALDEN: A LIFE IN THE WOODS. 1 vol. 16mo. Cloth. $1.00.

WARREN'S (DR. JOHN C.) LIFE. By Edward Warren, M. D. 2 vols. 8vo. $3.50.

" " THE PRESERVATION OF HEALTH. 1 vol. 38 cents.

WALLIS'S (S. T.) SPAIN AND HER INSTITUTIONS. 1 vol. 16mo. Cloth. $1.00.

WORDSWORTH'S (WILLIAM) BIOGRAPHY. By Dr. Christopher Wordsworth. 2 vols. 16mo. Cloth. $2.50.

WENSLEY: A STORY WITHOUT A MORAL. 1 vol. 16mo. Paper. 50 cents.

The Same. Cloth. 75 cents.

WHEATON'S (ROBERT) MEMOIRS. 1 vol. 16mo. Cloth. $1.00.

In Blue and Gold.

LONGFELLOW'S POETICAL WORKS. 2 vols. $1.75.

" PROSE WORKS. 2 vols. $1.75.

TENNYSON'S POETICAL WORKS. 2 vols. $1.50.

WHITTIER'S POETICAL WORKS. 2 vols. $1.50.

LEIGH HUNT'S POETICAL WORKS. 2 vols. $1.50.

GERALD MASSEY'S POETICAL WORKS. 1 vol. 75 cents.

MRS. JAMESON'S CHARACTERISTICS OF WOMEN. 75 cts.

" DIARY OF AN ENNUYEE. 1 vol. 75 cts.

" LOVES OF THE POETS. 1 vol. 75 cts.

" SKETCHES OF ART, &c. 1 vol. 75 cts.

" STUDIES AND STORIES. 1 vol. 75 cts.

" ITALIAN PAINTERS. 1 vol. 75 cents.

" LEGENDS OF THE MADONNA. 1 vol. 75 cents.

OWEN MEREDITH'S POEMS. 1 vol. 75 cents.

" LUCILE: A Poem. 1 vol. 75 cents.

BOWRING'S MATINS AND VESPERS. 1 vol. 75 cents.

LOWELL'S (J. RUSSELL) POETICAL WORKS. 2 vols. $1.50.

PERCIVAL'S POETICAL WORKS. 2 vols. $1.75.

MOTHERWELL'S POEMS. 1 vol. 75 cents.

SYDNEY DOBELL'S POEMS. 1 vol. 75 cents.

WILLIAM ALLINGHAM'S POEMS. 1 vol. 75 cents. *In Press.*

HORACE. Translated by Theodore Martin. 1 vol. 75 cts.

Works lately Published.

EDWIN OF DEIRA. By Alexander Smith, Author of "A Life Drama," &c. 1 vol. With fine Portrait of the Author. 75 cents.

THE AUTOBIOGRAPHY, LETTERS, AND LITERARY REMAINS OF MRS. THRALE PIOZZI. Edited by A. Hayward, Esq. 1 vol. $1.50.

THE LIFE AND CAREER OF MAJOR JOHN ANDRÉ. BY Winthrop Sargent. 1 vol. $1.50.

THE SABLE CLOUD. By Nehemiah Adams, D. D., Author of "A South-Side View of Slavery." 1 vol. 75 cents.

FAITHFUL FOREVER. By Coventry Patmore, Author of "The Angel in the House." 1 vol. $1.00.

OVER THE CLIFFS: A Novel. By Charlotte Chanter, (a sister of Rev. Charles Kingsley.) 1 vol. $1.00.

THE RECREATIONS OF A COUNTRY PARSON. 2 vols. $1.25 each. Sold together or separately.

REMINISCENCES OF SCOTTISH LIFE AND CHARACTER. By Dean Ramsay. From the Seventh Enlarged Edinburgh Edition. With an American Preface. 1 vol. 16mo. $1.00.

POEMS BY REV. WM. CROSWELL, D. D. Edited, with a Memoir, by Rev. Arthur Cleveland Coxe, D. D. 1 vol. $1.00.

PERSONAL HISTORY OF LORD BACON. From Original Letters and Documents. By Hepworth Dixon. 1 vol. $1.25.

POEMS. By Rose Terry. 1 vol. 16mo. 75 cents.

THE AUTOBIOGRAPHY OF THE REV. DR. ALEXANDER CARLYLE. Containing Memorials of the Men and Events of his Times. Edited by John Hill Burton.

FAVORITE AUTHORS: A Companion Book of Prose and Poetry. With 26 fine Steel Portraits. $2.50.

HEROES OF EUROPE. A capital Boy's Book. With 16 Illustrations. 1 vol. 16mo. $1.00.

BONNIE SCOTLAND. By Grace Greenwood. Illustrated. 75 cents.

THE SEVEN LITTLE SISTERS, who live in the Round Ball that floats in the Air. Illustrated. 63 cents.

www.ingramcontent.com/pod-product-compliance
Lightning Source LLC
LaVergne TN
LVHW050524100826
845148LV00002B/432
9781425520243